THE BOOK
OF
ST. BRIGID

COLM KEANE & UNA O'HAGAN

CAPEL
ISLAND

First published in Ireland in 2021

by

CAPEL ISLAND PRESS
Baile na nGall,
Ring, Dungarvan,
County Waterford,
Ireland

ISBN 978-1-9995920-3-5

Printed and bound by Clays Ltd, Elcograf S.p.A
Typesetting and cover design by Typeform Ltd

For Seán and Ned

Colm Keane has published 29 books, including eight No.1 chart bestsellers, among them *The Little Flower: St. Thérèse of Lisieux, Padre Pio: Irish Encounters with the Saint, Going Home, We'll Meet Again* and *Heading for the Light.* He is a graduate of Trinity College, Dublin, and Georgetown University, Washington D.C. As a broadcaster, he won a Jacob's Award and a Glaxo Fellowship for European Science Writers.

Una O'Hagan is a No.1 bestselling author and former news-reader with Radio Telefís Éireann. A DIT journalism graduate, she has interviewed Nelson Mandela, accompanied President Mary Robinson on a state visit to Australia and hosted live programmes on the deaths of former Taoisigh Jack Lynch and Garret FitzGerald and the state visit of Queen Elizabeth II to Ireland. This is her fourth book.

CONTENTS

Saint Brigid

The dandelion lights its spark
Lest Brigid find the wayside dark,
And Brother Wind comes rollicking
For joy that she has brought the spring
Young lambs and little furry folk
Seek shelter underneath her cloak.

Winifred M. Letts (1882 – 1972)

INTRODUCTION

This is a book about an abbess, monastery founder, miracle worker and saint who, in the fifth and sixth centuries, wielded more power in the Catholic Church than any woman has wielded before or since. Not only did she set up one of the most successful and innovative monasteries in history, but her convents were scattered all over Ireland. Her fame also spread down through the centuries.

Today, numerous Irish churches, schools, holy wells and parish halls are named after her. So, also, are family surnames like MacBride, Bride and Kilbride. The same is true for place-names like Rathbride, Toberbride, Brides Glen and Kilbride, not to mention the gossipy people we refer to as "old biddies" and places of detention we call Bridewells.

Thousands of girls and women bear her name. There have been, and still are, a lot of them about – many named Brigid or Bridget; others named Bridie, Breege, Bríd, Bride, Biddy, Breda, Bid, or even Bee and Beesy. There was a time when you could hardly round a corner in Ireland without bumping into one of them.

Oliver Cromwell named his daughter Bridget. Another Bridget, from Ireland, became sister-in-law to Adolf Hitler. Brigitte Bardot made her name famous internationally. Maud Gonne MacBride adopted her as her patron saint. So, too, did the women workers during the 1913 lockout. Lady Gregory wrote a play about her.

In modern times, Aer Lingus has named planes after her. Telefís Éireann chose her cross as its symbol. The Brigidine Sisters

1

continue to implement her monastic traditions. A famous flower bears her name. Even the tiered wedding cake owes its inspiration to her, as does the Rosary beads. All these stories you will read about in this book.

She is also remembered abroad – at St. Brides Bay in Wales, St. Bees Head in Cumbria, even in the Hebrides in Scotland, whose name is said to derive from hers. There is a St. Brigid's school in Tasmania, a Bride Peak in the Himalayan Mountains, and an island named Bride off the coast of Japan.

People down through the ages have prayed to her for help. She has been variously named as the patron saint of milkmaids, farm animals, cattle farmers, midwives, nuns, newborn babies, mariners, poets, the poor, students and travellers, and lots more. As you will see, there is good reason why she is also one of the patron saints of brewers.

Her omnipresence in these less religious times may often go unnoticed, but she is always there – in the names of people we meet, villages we pass through, churches we enter, halls we frequent, sports clubs we support, and schools to which we send our children.

She is worthy of the recognition as, by all accounts, she was a kind-hearted woman, modest, humble, an animal lover, with no pretensions to power or fame. A friend to the poor and untiringly charitable, her avowed desire was to relieve human despair.

Hers is the story of a woman who rose from little or nothing, achieved greatness in her life, won over the hearts of a nation, and set an example for standards of kindness, charity and decency rare even among saints. We hope the following pages remind you of why she is worth remembering.

THE EARLY YEARS

A few miles from Dundalk, overlooking Dundalk Bay, there is a lofty hill with spectacular views over the surrounding terrain. In the distance, to the north and east, lie the Cooley Mountains, while below and away to the far horizon can be seen the plains of the south and the sparkling waters of the Irish Sea.

Fifteen hundred years ago, this site, known as Faughart Hill, marked the home of a chieftain named Dubthach – known as Duffy today – and his bondswoman Brocessa. It was here, around the year 450, their daughter Brigid was born.

Legend tells us that the child was predicted to become "full of grace before God and man" and that her name would be "celebrated throughout the entire world." As we will see in the following chapter, those predictions came to pass.

Brigid showed a marked independence of character when she was growing up. This feature stood to her in her later life as the Abbess of Kildare.

There is an insightful story told about Brigid when she was young. Once she was old enough, she was given the job of churning the cows' milk on her father's farm. This she did in the company of other women. At day's end, they would deliver the fruits of their labour, to be weighed at an appointed time.

Brigid had a problem – she couldn't stop herself giving things to the poor. She was doing it all the time, handing a sheep out here, some milk there, or any object she could lay her hands on. On this day, nothing was different. She liberally handed out butter and milk to those in need, and by day's end had nothing to show for her work.

"She had given the lot away to the poor without a thought for the morrow," the monk Cogitosus, who wrote little more than a century after Brigid's death and most likely lived at her monastery in Kildare, remarked. She dreaded her mother's response, he said, so she got down on her knees and prayed.

"Without delay, the Lord heard the maiden's voice and prayers. And, being a helper in the hour of need, he came to her assistance with the generous bestowal of a divine gift, and lavishly restored the butter for the maiden who had confidence in him," Cogitosus said. It was one of the earliest miracles associated with Brigid.

By all accounts, Brigid was a beautiful girl, both physically and in spirit. Her figure was moulded with an unusual gracefulness, and she was of bright mind, according to early accounts. She had a ready smile, and her looks were said to be angelic. Many people remarked on her propriety of speech and her interest in holy practices.

Everyone noticed her personal holiness. They observed how, as a young child, she set up her own altar from a smooth slab of stone. Four wooden legs held it up having been put there by an angel, it was later said. People also noticed her politeness and modesty. Although always joyful, she often blushed.

Despite these endearing qualities, she was headstrong and independent. Like the later saints Thérèse of Lisieux and Bernadette of Lourdes, she knew her own mind and never deviated. In this respect, she was true to her name, which meant "power," "strength" and "vigour." No one was more determined to achieve her goals than the future Abbess of Kildare.

From an early age, strange things happened around Brigid. On one occasion, when she was minding her father's pigs, they broke apart as a herd and dispersed over a wide distance. Two unscrupulous men noticed what was happening, stole two of them, and began to lead them away.

To their surprise, her father approached from nearby. On seeing him, the robbers fled, leaving the pigs behind. Recognising that they belonged to him, her father concealed the two pigs and approached Brigid asking if she could account for the whole herd.

Brigid suggested he should count them, pointing to all those under her control. This he agreed to do. He counted, and he counted, and he counted again, and none of the pigs was missing. There was clearly something different about Brigid!

Early miracles were also associated with her love of animals, especially dogs. At one time, she was cooking bacon in a cauldron for some guests who had arrived at her father's house. Suddenly, she heard the whining of a hungry dog begging for food. Unable to resist, she gave it a sizeable portion of the bacon to eat.

Once again, the problem was solved. "When the bacon was taken from the cauldron and later divided among the guests, it was found perfectly intact as if none of it had been taken away," Cogitosus remarked. Those who knew what she had done yet witnessed the outcome "were full of admiration," he wrote.

This inner desire – even compulsion – to be charitable was something she carried with her for the rest of her life. On one occasion, after she had become a nun, she was asked to select one of the eight beatitudes as a subject for devotion.

Brigid hardly thought for a moment before making her choice. "Mercy," she said, identifying straight away those characteristics of compassion, pity and kindness that she had carried with her since her days as a child.

It was also the driving force behind her decision to become a nun. She was impelled not only by her desire to serve God but by her need "to comfort the poor, to banish all distress, to relieve all wretchedness," the late 15th-century text, the *Book of Lismore*, noted of her character. Her father, though, had different ideas.

Following a not uncommon practice at the time, he decided to sell Brigid as a slave. Approaching the King of Leinster, he explained that his decision was based on the fear he would become destitute as she gave all he owned to the poor.

The king, whose aides made him aware of the young girl's virtues, was surprised. He asked to see Brigid, who was waiting outside. Her father went to collect her, only to discover that while she was waiting she had given his precious sword to a man who was poor.

Enraged, he explained this latest transgression to the king, who was more impressed than shocked. Looking straight at her father, he said that Brigid was "too holy and exalted to be either bought or sold." She was "more precious than any amount of silver or gold," he added.

Take her home, the king said, presenting her father with another sword as a substitute for the one gone missing. Thanks to that intervention, Brigid's path ahead was secured and her fate was sealed. From then on, she devoted herself to prayer, undertook vigils and fasting, and prepared herself for the one thing she wished above all other – to become a nun.

When she was 16 years of age, Brigid set out to be professed as a nun. She ended up becoming a bishop.

Croghan Hill is a small, isolated hill rising from the Bog of Allen in County Offaly. Its green slopes contrast sharply with the black-brown hue of the surrounding bog. Today, it is hard to get to. At the time of Brigid, it was a much more difficult journey.

Back then, Croghan Hill was approached by wooden track-ways cut into the vast, low-lying expanse of bog. It was along these trackways that Brigid, aged 16, and seven of her companions travelled on their way to a church on the hill's eastern slopes.

She expected that Bishop Mel, who tradition tells us was a nephew of St. Patrick, would be there. He was a churchman of influence and importance. He was the right man, Brigid believed, to receive her into the Church as a nun.

Brigid was greatly disappointed when told that Mel was elsewhere. She spoke to a pupil of his, named Mac Caille, who informed her that the bishop was in Westmeath. "The way is trackless, with marshes, deserts, bogs and pools," he warned. She decided to go there anyway.

The following day, Mac Caille and the eight women headed north to meet Bishop Mel. On arrival, Mac Caille informed him that the women wished to be professed as nuns. As Mel looked at them, it was said that a column of fire shone above Brigid's head.

Mel asked: "Who is she?" Mac Caille told him who she was. The bishop immediately recognised her. He had known her parents. "It is I who foretold her future, when she was in her mother's womb," he said, referring to a vision he once had of Brigid. He then agreed to perform the ceremony.

Brigid wore a white cloak and had a white veil over her head. The other women were also dressed in white. At her own request, out of humility, Brigid was the last to be professed. It was then that something extraordinary happened.

The ancient manuscript, the *Liber Hymnorum*, recounts in detail what occurred. This book of hymns, whose contents date back to as early as the sixth century, is clear that "the episcopal order" – meaning the title of bishop – was conferred on Brigid.

"It came to pass that Bishop Mel conferred on Brigit the episcopal order," the author of the text wrote. "And hence Brigit's successor is always entitled to have episcopal orders and the honour due to a bishop."

The ninth-century *Bethu Brigte* concurs with this view. The manuscript, largely written in Irish, details how Mel "consecrated Brigit with the orders of a bishop." It goes on to say that "this virgin alone in Ireland will hold the episcopal ordination."

The *Book of Lismore* drives home the point. "The form of ordaining a bishop was read out over Brigit," it says. Mac Caille then tried to correct Bishop Mel, saying that "a bishop's order should not be conferred on a woman." The bishop replied: "No power have I in this matter. That dignity has been given by God unto Brigit, beyond every (other) woman."

This latter book, the *Book of Lismore* – one of the great books of Ireland – concluded that from then on "the men of Ireland" would be obliged not only to regard Brigid as a bishop but that "Brigit's successor" would also hold the title.

And that's exactly what happened. Not only was Brigid referred to as "bishop" but her sisters succeeding her as Abbess of Kildare shared in that honour. It wasn't until the 11th and 12th centuries that everything changed.

Not only were women, from then on, prevented from attaining the office but attempts were made to eradicate memories of such ordinations in the past. Thus began the era when the Church became a fiercely-guarded male preserve.

Few issues concerning Brigid have caused more controversy over the years than the question of whether she was, or was not, ordained a bishop. Two sides to the debate are identifiable: one representing mostly male, conservative Catholic traditionalists who are hostile to the idea; the other representing academics or females – or, much more importantly, the authors of the ancient texts reviewed above – who believe it to be true.

One hostile commentator – a convert to Catholicism who edited a Catholic newspaper – called the proposition a "grotesque fable." Another argued that the bishop who ordained her "did not recognise what he was reciting from his book." It was also alleged that he was drunk. More claimed that what happened must have been "accidental."

Yet, according to the multiple unfettered early accounts we saw above, which recorded what happened closer to the time, the fact of the matter is simple – Brigid was ordained a bishop, and a bishop she remained for the rest of her life.

Having set up smaller convents in various parts of Ireland, Brigid eventually arrived in Kildare, where she built one of the finest monastic settlements in ecclesiastical history.

Each evening, from December to December, for more than 1,000 years, the nuns at the convent in Kildare kept alight an "inextinguishable" fire. As darkness fell, through fair and foul weather, a nun would approach the blaze and use bellows or a pitchfork and not her breath to rekindle it, keeping it going for the next 24 hours. The process was repeated each day.

The fire was surrounded by a circular hedge of long, thin willow stems, across which no male dared to tread. "If by chance one does dare to enter – and some rash people have at times tried it – he does not escape the divine vengeance," we are told by Gerald of Wales, who witnessed the fire and described it in the mid-1180s.

That the fire lasted so long – up to the 16th century – tells us much about the ultimate size, longevity and resilience of the monastery begun by Brigid in Kildare. It became so big and influential that, within a short span of time, the monastic settlement was being described as "a vast metropolitan city."

The location she chose was ideal. At the time, it was a continual forest, save in one part where there was a gentle undulating plain known as the Curragh. The plain was "a pastoral tract of unusual beauty and extent," it was said. The edge of the forest held another attraction: a majestic oak tree, which Brigid loved and blessed.

It was there she decided to build her first monastic huts. She was joined by all seven nuns she had been ordained with. Others soon joined up. They all wore white, we are told, although a cloak said to have been Brigid's, which is held in Bruges, is coloured red or purplish blue, perhaps reflecting her status as a bishop.

As the community grew larger and the cells became more numerous, the monastery was obliged to widen its bounds. The few fields pasturing the sheep and cows were no longer sufficient, and a wider expanse of land was required. The local landowners were helpful, it seems, although one proved obstinate.

An amusing legend tells us that one day she was standing with the landlord on a mound overlooking the Curragh. He was refusing to grant more land to the monastery. "At any rate," the abbess said, "will you give me as much ground as my cloak will cover?" He could hardly say no.

The four sisters who accompanied Brigid immediately took hold of her cloak and fled north, south, east and west, covering more and more ground as they ran. The owner, who was thrown into a state of consternation, appealed to Brigid to call them back before they covered the whole of Ireland. She got her way, and her land was expanded, the legend says.

The monastery eventually housed men and women, living side by side. The males, who were monks, lived in one community; the nuns lived in another. It was, in that sense, a double monastery, unique in Ireland and a model for monasteries overseas. And it wasn't just prayer and contemplation that was practised; lots of work was done, too.

The place was a hive of activity. The nuns farmed the lands, tended the herds and flocks, spun and weaved, amassed a library of manuscripts, maintained a guest house, schools, hospital and dispensary, and embroidered vestments. It would take 900 years before anything like it would emerge on the Continent.

The Curragh was the community's pasture ground. The sheep were cared for and protected. Their wool was shorn and made into habits and other nuns' garments. The cows were fed and milked. Nuns worked in the dairy, where butter and cheese were made. Every day, the large numbers of poor people who sought alms were attended to.

The sizeable infirmary was the prototype of a modern hospital. With its vast supply of herb mixtures, the nuns running it looked after the sick poor. They also taught in the schools, where students flocked from all over the country. Others worked in the scriptorium, copying and illuminating manuscripts.

A great *Book of Kildare* was designed and written there, according to Gerald of Wales, who saw it. The secrets of the artistry, the images, the colourings, the intricate details were such that "all these things must have been the result of the work, not of men, but of angels," he wrote. Unfortunately, the *Book of Kildare* disappeared a long time ago, probably pillaged by invaders.

The settlement expanded so rapidly that another person of authority was required to help oversee it. Bishop Conlaeth, a recluse, who had been famous as a metalworker before he became a priest, was chosen. Under his guidance, the monks made chalices, bells, crosiers, patens, bookrests and shrines, which were used in the monastery and distributed elsewhere.

The site also boasted a wonderful cathedral for contemplation and prayer. We are fortunate that a first-hand description of the building was chronicled by the monk Cogitosus.

He tells us that the cathedral was divided into two portions by a wooden screen or partition, which ran down the whole length of the building. On one side sat the abbess, the nuns and other females. On the other side sat the bishop, clergy and males. Each side had its own door.

The cathedral was spectacular, spacious and "elevated to a marvellous height." Painted figures decorated the walls, and tapestries were hung on the partitions. The church was always full during services, which were solemnly and edifyingly performed by clerics specially selected by Brigid.

It was here, at the centre of this massive monastic complex, that Brigid reigned supreme. The project could hardly have been going better. The respect she was getting as Abbess of Kildare was unmatched. But Brigid had bigger plans, and she was soon on the road, travelling to territories far afield, realising her broader monastic dream.

Brigid established numerous monasteries while travelling the length and breadth of Ireland. She ended up in charge of more than 10,000 nuns.

A story is told about the time Brigid crossed the River Shannon having sorted out problems at some of her monasteries in Connaught. She and her sisters were on their way home. Arriving at Athlone, they were obliged to cross the Shannon, which was the boundary between the ancient provinces of Connaught and Meath.

A few of her sisters approached boatmen who were idle on the shore and asked if they might ferry them across. The boatmen insisted on being paid unreasonable sums of money; others claim it was valuable clothing they demanded. Either way, they weren't doing the job for free.

The nuns were indignant and walked away. They turned instead to Brigid and asked that she make a Sign of the Cross over the Shannon waters. They hoped the act might lower the waters and make the river fordable. This she did.

Brigid and her sisters entered the river and began to wade across. The waters sank and never reached more than knee-high. They made it to the other side. Everyone who watched was amazed. All present "gave glory to God," it was said.

Brigid not only entered Connaught, where she set up monasteries, but she also travelled to the plains of Limerick, to Waterford,

Tipperary and Kerry, including a necklace of locations along the shores of the Irish Sea from Tramore to Bray. She founded monasteries in many of these locations.

These were tough journeys at the time. She travelled on rough roads, traversed great rivers, drove through valleys and glens, avoided big woods of oak and ash, while all the time alert to the danger of foxes, red wolves, boars and bears. Some rivers she crossed were leaping with salmon; others were treacherous beyond compare.

She and her companions stayed in humble houses or, if lucky, hospitality might be offered by a person of rank. A bishop's invitation would be gratefully accepted. In this latter case, the bishop, clerics and nuns would sit down to a fine meal, occasionally complemented by the delivery of poetry and song.

The work was tough. Everything had to be started from scratch. Religious vocations needed to be secured, churches and monasteries built, spiritual values fostered in the local population. Altar drapes had to be woven and priests' vestments embroidered. Chalices wrought in precious metal, sweet-toned bells hammered in bronze, and ornate tabernacles had to be found.

Brigid was fortunate in her mode of transport. She travelled in what was called a *carbad*, or "chariot," which was a cab made of wicker, with an outer frame of wooden bars. Drawn by horses, it was often decorated with tin. Her driver was her priest, Natfroich, who seemed to accompany her almost everywhere she went.

There were many mishaps along the way. On one occasion, she fell from the chariot and her head was cut open. On another occasion, her driver – not Natfroich this time – took a shortcut home through private lands which were in the process of being fenced.

The workers doing the fencing objected, resulting in the driver stepping down from the carriage and engaging in a free-for-all with the men. Brigid had to separate the combatants, which she did successfully, it seems.

Natfroich was back as charioteer when she had another mishap. This one happened when she was being driven to the plain of the Liffey. Another sister was with her, and the chariot was being pulled by two horses.

The priest was regaling his two passengers about a matter of spiritual importance. He kept turning his head over his shoulder. After a while, Brigid said: "Turn round that we may hear better, and throw down the reins." He took her advice.

No one noticed that one of the horses, a short while later, slipped free from the yoke. The carriage, as a result, ran on one side, right on the edge of a dangerous precipice. Somehow, the remaining horse worked wonders and the day was saved. People said it was miraculous that a catastrophe was averted.

The people of Leinster were never pleased with Brigid's travels. They were aware that her fame was spreading all over Ireland and that vast numbers of people were being drawn to her wherever she went. Worried that she may never come back, they sent a delegation to entice her to revisit her native province.

They obviously picked the right moment. She may well have been tired of life on the road. She may equally have had desires to develop her monastic project closer to the place of her birth. Whatever the reason, Brigid was soon on her way back to Kildare, and it was there she would base herself for the rest of her life.

At Kildare, Brigid liked nothing better than caring for her sheep. She did so on the vast, rolling expanse of the Curragh.

During bitter, frost-clad days or tepid summer nights, Brigid could be seen caring for her sheep on the plains of the Curragh. There, amid the flat grasslands, low-lying hills and glowing furze blossoms, she could be found contemplating God and protecting her flocks from harm.

She loved few things better than her sheep. References to them are chronicled in many ancient texts. A legendary poem by St. Cuimin of Connor, who flourished in the seventh century, revealed that apart from Brigid's "constant piety," her main features were "sheep herding and early rising." Tradition sometimes referred to her as "The Shepherdess."

She had learned her trade as a young girl. The *Book of Lismore* records how, when she was young, "she tended the sheep, she satisfied the birds, she fed the poor." She performed all the other jobs that a young farm girl might do, including grinding the corn and washing the feet of guests. But it was her main jobs that mattered most – tending the sheep on the mountain and herding the animals on the farm.

She brought her farm skills with her to her convent life. She understood the backbreaking work during harvest time. She knew what it was like to carry a churn, or milk the cows in the morning and evening. She was familiar with the skill of kneading dough for bread. She was proficient in the art of shearing sheep, so that their wool would clothe her companions.

She could also put up with bad weather. One legend recalls how, after a full day of drenching rain, she returned to the convent saturated to her skin. It happened that a visitor was lecturing to

16

the sisters at the time. Caught up in what he was saying, Brigid forgot to change her clothes. Legend tells us that a sunbeam entered her cell and the clothes were dried by divine intervention.

Many interesting stories – sometimes referred to as "miracles" – were gathered regarding Brigid's time as a shepherdess. One story, widely recorded, recalls how a young man who was rich decided to pull a trick and relieve her of some sheep. Knowing she was kind-hearted, he approached her one day in one of the fields, dressed as a pauper.

He arrived bearing a staff, his walk unsteady, his voice cracked, his breathing laboured, and he asked her for a sheep. Noting his condition, she gave him one, which he took with him. Buoyed by his success, he returned in another disguise and repeated his request. She gave him another. The trick was repeated no less than seven times.

Her companions, on hearing what happened, were baffled when they discovered that the original sheep were present when the flock was counted in the evening. The trickster was even more baffled when he discovered that the seven sheep he had so cleverly acquired were gone. The joke was on him, we are informed, which annoyed him to the core.

Another story was told concerning her cattle. Two robbers stole cattle from her field and led them away. Everything was going well until they reached a river, which had to be crossed. The cattle refused to ford the river. No amount of shouting or beating would induce them to do so. All night long the robbers tried to move them, but to no avail.

The following morning, the robbers conjured up a brilliant plan. They took off their clothes, tied the clothes to the animals' horns to keep them dry, fixed ropes to the cattle, and pulled them into the river. Halfway across, the cattle decided they would take no more. They broke away from the ropes and headed back the way they had come.

The cattle bolted for home, with the clothes still tied to their horns. It was reported that onlookers were treated to the spectacle of two naked men wildly pursuing the cattle, trailing a long distance behind them. The onlookers were "wondrously amazed," it was noted.

It is no surprise that Brigid, following her farming exploits, ended up being invoked as the protector of farm animals. This was so not only in Ireland but abroad. The early 20th-century Breton Benedictine, Dom Louis Gougaud, identified four parochial churches and seven chapels in the diocese of Cologne which were dedicated to Brigid and under whose protection the local farmers placed their animals.

The town of Fosses in northern France was the same. There, the "peasantry also come to invoke the saint's aid for their livestock in the chapel dedicated to her," Dom Gougaud noted. Similar devotion pertained in Portugal, where local residents around the small Portuguese parish of Lumiar commended their sheep and cattle to her protection.

In Ireland, perhaps the greatest farming legacy she has left behind is the almost 5,000-acre commonage for grazing sheep at the Curragh in County Kildare. The rights of commonage there originated with Brigid. Today, the grasslands echo to the quiet stillness of those days and nights when she protected her sheep more than 1,500 years ago.

Over the years, the Kildare monastery hosted numerous guests who needed to be watered and fed. Brigid was lucky as she had an accomplished if long-suffering cook to cater for them. Her name was Flora.

One day, "certain religious men" arrived at Brigid's monastery in Kildare, where they preached the Divine Word. They were, we are told, "pious guests." Once their preaching was over, Brigid asked her cook, Flora, to make dinner. "What kind of a meal should be prepared?" Flora asked. Brigid replied: "Give them bread and butter, with several dishes of meat and onions."

Flora headed to the cellar to collect the food. Not for the first time, there was nothing there. She must have sighed in despair. Brigid, she discovered, had given everything to the poor. A panic-stricken Flora returned to Brigid and advised her that it would be best if she retired to the church to pray. "We will have to trust the result to Divine Providence," the cook said.

Brigid sprang into action, saying, "Why don't you sweep the kitchen floor, close the cookhouse, then go to your own house and pray. I will go to the church." The two parted and went their separate ways. Coming up to six o'clock – the time for the meal – Brigid sent for Flora and said: "The time for waiting on our guests has arrived; go now to the cellar, and liberally give them whatever you may find there."

Flora did as she was instructed. On entering the cellar, she discovered that it was full of all the kinds of food requested by Brigid. Copious supplies of bread, butter, various meats and onions filled the cellar's shelves. Not only was there more than enough food for the meal, but the supplies fed the guests, the whole community, and even the poor for a full seven days.

We are informed that, at the time, no one knew where the food had come from or who had provided it. "Knowledge of this miraculous occurrence remained among the secrets of Divine Omnipotence," it was later remarked. We can only hope that the tolerant, uncomplaining, stoical – perhaps even resigned – Flora received at least some of the credit!

By all accounts, Flora was a wonderful person, known for her heroic sanctity and devotion to Brigid. Hers was a busy job. She had a lot of mouths to feed and a lot of visitors to provide for. She would labour every day in her kitchen, baking wheat and barley breads, making the curd-cheese, cooking the meats, and preparing delightful fruit salads of apples, blackberries and nuts.

We don't know much about her, including where she came from or what she was like. We do know that her original name was Bláth, meaning "flower," which translates from the Irish to Flora, the name by which she is commonly referred to today. We also know from ancient texts that she was an important figure in the monastery. The other thing we can deduce is that she had plenty of problems to deal with.

Her biggest headache was Brigid, who couldn't stop giving to the poor. She gave with abandon. On one occasion, she was given a basket of high-quality apples as a gift. She immediately spotted a group of sick people and, opening the basket, gave the apples to them. "I didn't bring the apples for them, but for you," the lady who had arrived with the gift said. Brigid replied: "What is mine is theirs."

Another time, several ecclesiastical notables were expected to arrive at the monastery and Flora and her assistants scurried about preparing the finest dishes. Before their arrival, a group of beggars came looking for food. Brigid, as usual, viewed them with compassion and handed over the carefully-prepared feast, down to the last crumb.

That wonderful seventh-century monk Cogitosus reminds us, however, that unlike most housewives or cooks, Flora had one thing on her side – Brigid's miraculous powers. One day, he said, bishops arrived at the monastery, but the place was out of milk. There was none to give them and no prospect of finding any as only one cow was available.

Brigid was up to the task. She milked the cow three times that day, and it produced more than enough milk to refresh the bishops and everyone else besides. Miraculously, and contrary to the laws of nature, the cow furnished the same amount of milk as three of her best cows usually produced. Flora, we can presume, was pleased.

The 17th-century Italian abbot, Giacomo Certani, tells us of another miraculous outcome, this time involving a dog. It seems that while Flora was busy preparing food in the kitchen, the dog crept in and stole a large piece of bacon. Everyone looked for it, but it couldn't be found. After a month, it was discovered untouched and in perfect condition in the dog's kennel.

Perhaps thanks to fortunate outcomes like these, Flora seems to have lived a long life, and she died just a few years before Brigid. She is remembered for her ability to always put food on the table and to turn ordinary tasks into something extraordinary. For those talents alone, and perhaps for the agony she went through – the stress and tension caused by Brigid – she, like her boss, ended up in the register of saints. It's the least she deserved!

Kerry-born St. Brendan, or "Brendan the Navigator" as he is often called, was among those who knew and visited Brigid. One of his visits provided a rare insight to Brigid's holiness.

There is a charming story of a meeting between Brendan and Brigid in Leinster. He travelled, we are told, all the way "from the West of Ireland" to see her. Arriving at her monastery, he found she wasn't there. He waited, and he waited, and he waited. Eventually, she "came from her sheep to welcome Brendan," the medieval *Leabhar Breac* – the "Speckled Book" – informs us.

At the time, Brigid was Mother Abbess of thousands of nuns. "One would have expected a personage of such importance to have been discovered at some more impressive employment: seated on a rostrum, perhaps, haranguing her community, or exhorting them; or at a desk before a manuscript, with a quill pen in her hand," Alice Curtayne, the St. Brigid expert, wrote in 1933.

Everything we need to know about Brigid is told in that line about her being with her sheep, Curtayne remarked. Where she found shelter, where her strength was secretly renewed, where her soul found peace, was in the solitude of "the green fields under the open sky." Hence that picture of Arcadian beauty in the simple words: "Brigit came from her sheep to welcome Brendan."

On the other hand, it was a tribute to Brigid that Brendan should have waited so long. Of all the seafarers of Fenit, eight miles west of Tralee, where he was born, he was known as the toughest and bravest of them all. He was particularly known for taking on the rough-crested seas, billowing tides and restless currents of the Atlantic in his quest to find "the land of promise of the saints."

Brendan was no less formidable on land. He chose for his oratory an inaccessible mountain peak, 3,000 feet above the sea, which was battered by vicious Atlantic gales. He was also founder of a number of monasteries, including two notable foundations at Clonfert and Ardfert.

Interestingly, one of his monasteries, Annaghdown, on Lough Corrib, although initially for nuns, seems to have eventually taken on both male and female religious, just as Brigid's had done. That monastery was run by Brendan's sister, Briga, whose name was a derivative of Brigid.

Although Brendan clearly admired Brigid, it was strange to find such a redoubtable man paying her a visit. "It is really rather surprising to find this indomitable explorer, who was more practised in seamanship than in conversation with nuns, this restless adventurer for God, this most audacious of the saints, admitting that he had something to learn from Brigid," Alice Curtayne remarked.

The visit, we can deduce, was inspired either directly or indirectly by Bishop Erc of Slane. Otherwise known as Eric or Ercus, he was a friend of Brigid and had once accompanied her to Munster, where he had relatives. He was also the tutor of Brendan, who he would later ordain as a priest. Bishop Erc always spoke highly of Brigid and her miraculous powers, which perhaps prompted the meeting.

We can visualise Brendan as he met Brigid, his face tanned from the sun, his eyes alert and focused from life at sea. He had waited for her, he said, to ask her a question of profound importance – to what degree did she love God? Before answering, Brigid asked him to tell her how much *he* loved God. She would then reply, she said.

"From the day I entered upon a devout life I never went over seven furrows without my mind being on God," Brendan told her. Given that a furrow represented a narrow trench in the ground for sowing seeds, the time involved was short, indeed. Then Brigid replied: "For my part, since I first applied my mind to God, I have never for a moment diverted my attention from Him."

For Brendan, her response was said to have been edifying and transformative; one of profound moral and intellectual significance. For a woman who did so much, met so many people, managed so many lives, and travelled to places so far afield, she had never – not even "for a moment" – lost sight of God.

Various versions of the encounter have been recorded over time. While many colourful scenarios have been documented, the likelihood is that the conversation between the two future saints was as described above. It certainly left its mark on Brendan who, one old text tells us, having received Brigid's blessing, and given his in return, left an enlightened man.

If only as a result of their meeting, it is no surprise to find in the *Liber Hymnorum* – the book of ancient Irish Church hymns, held by Trinity College – that Brendan is credited as one of the possible composers of a wonderful hymn dedicated to Brigid. The first few lines of the introductory quatrain are both simple and beautiful.

"Brigid, excellent woman, a flame golden, delightful; may she, the sun dazzling, splendid, guide us to the eternal kingdom," the text reads. Those few lines, composed so long ago, tell us all we need to know about how much he respected Brigid, having waited for her to come from her sheep and answer his question all those years before.

Brigid, who was an expert at brewing ale, made sure that copious supplies of the product were made available to her visitors. She later became one of the patron saints of brewers.

Brigid's talents at manufacturing ale were legendary. She was noted not only for the quality of her ale but for ensuring it was readily available to her guests. Visiting churchmen, alms-seekers, the poor, the infirm, availed of her largesse. They might have been right to do so as her product was made from the finest ingredients grown in the rich farmlands of County Kildare.

Brigid used local barley cultivated in perfect soil and climatic conditions as her main ingredient. Hops, which were not grown in Ireland at the time, were missing. Hence her product was not beer but "ale." Either way, we can visualise Brigid and her sisters grounding, mashing, fermenting, boiling, straining, and serving her high-quality, homemade brew.

That Brigid brewed ale is not as strange as it sounds. The drink was commonly consumed in Ireland at the time. It was safer and cleaner than water, a good source of nutrition, calories and hydration, and was much lower in alcohol compared to the beers or ales on the market today. It was also a time when tea was unavailable – that didn't arrive in Ireland until more than 1,000 years later. In its absence, ale filled the gap admirably.

"Ale was the universal drink and was always offered to visitors in much the same way as a cup of tea is offered now," the St. Brigid expert Alice Curtayne wrote. "Being hardly fermented, its intoxicating properties were negligible. One need not, therefore, grudge the Celtic monks their ration of ale......Our modern tea is probably a more stimulating and a far less wholesome beverage than the fifth-century ale."

Brigid was familiar with the drink as a young girl, we are told in the *Book of Lismore*. A tale documented in the manuscript concerns a journey she made while still a "handmaid." Brigid was travelling in the company of a nurse, the document, written in Irish, tells us. An unforeseen incident took place, culminating in a miraculous outcome:

"Illness seized her nurse as she was wending her way. So Brigit and another girl were sent to ask a drink of ale for her from a certain man named Baethchu, who was making a mighty feast. He refused Brigit. Then Brigit went to a certain well, and filled her vessel thereat, and blessed (the water), so that it turned into the taste of ale, and she gave it to her nurse, who straight-away became whole."

Brigid never lost sight of the importance of manufacturing and distributing ale during her time in charge of her monastic settlements. The *Book of Lismore*, once again, chronicles how she mass-produced the drink for distribution to "the many churches that were around her." The area included the territory of the Fir Tulach ("Men of the Hills") in ancient Meath, in the heart of the midlands.

On one occasion, the manuscript informs us, she faced a shortage of ingredients – both corn and malt – and a shortage of vats, threatening her supplies to that area. She resolved the problem miraculously, meeting the needs of 17 churches out of one measure of malt, providing them with enough ale to last "from Maundy Thursday to Low Sunday." That the supply lasted for such a long period of time around Easter – 11 days – was believed to be miraculous.

Ale featured in another Brigid miracle, this time involving the surprise arrival at her monastery of Bishop Mac Caille, from Offaly, and a large retinue of clerics. When preparing to feed them, she discovered that apart from water she had only a small quantity of ale available. Worried by the predicament, she wondered what to do.

"She made a Sign of the Cross over the beverage, when it was miraculously increased, so as to satisfy more than the wants of all her assembled guests," the Rev. John O'Hanlon tells us in his renowned *Lives of the Irish Saints*. As a result, several vessels were filled with the contents of the single vessel, thereby resolving the problem.

"The bishop and his clerics departed, after having experienced the hospitality of their pious hostess, and even more gratified because of her merits and the miracle she wrought, than with any corporeal entertainment she afforded them," O'Hanlon remarked.

Brigid was equally distressed when a group of paupers came to her requesting a draught of ale. They were thirsty, they explained. Unfortunately, she didn't have any ale to give them. While thinking about what to do, she spotted, a short distance away, water that had been prepared for baths.

Once again, she made a Sign of the Cross over the water and, as the legend tells us, it was transformed into ale. "Brigid rejoiced when she had been enabled to present the thirsting multitude of poor with ale instead of water, thus satisfying both their requests and their necessities. Thus, she seemed never to tire in bestowing largesses on the poor and wretched," O'Hanlon concluded.

We cannot be sure, of course, of the veracity of these miracles, some or all of which may be exaggerated in an attempt to inflate Brigid's holiness. They may, equally, be true. What we do know, however, is that Brigid was a master brewer in her time, producing ale for her community, guests and outlying monasteries.

We also know that her ale was popular and of the highest quality. As Guinness pointed out in a guidebook from 1928, the brew she produced was the "drink of the people," admirably and professionally brewed by her, the saint of the people.....and Guinness, if anyone, should know!

Brigid's holiness became so widely known that numerous people approached her seeking help. They did so more than ever when news of her miracles spread throughout the land. The following is a sample of those miracles, as documented in ancient texts.

One day, a woman came to visit Brigid, accompanied by her 12-year-old daughter. The young girl had been without speech since birth. Unaware of her affliction, Brigid took the girl's hand and spoke to her. Wondering what she wished to do with her life, she asked if she'd like to become a nun or maybe get married.

The girl, lacking speech, never replied. Her mother explained why. Brigid said to the mother: "I will not let go of the girl's hand until she gives me an answer." She then turned once more to the girl and kindly asked her what she wanted to do. Instantly, she replied: "I do not want to do anything except what you want." Afterwards, we are told, the girl was able to speak normally and without impediment.

Brigid's cures and revivals were legendary. She was said to have healed paralytics, those who were blind, and people with upset minds. She showed particular concern for sufferers from leprosy, the scourge of the time, with no known cure. She also showed compassion to couples going through fragile marriages, helping them to reconcile.

On one occasion, during a visit to a nearby monastery, she encountered a nun who was paralysed. "Please pray to Christ for me that I may be healed," the nun pleaded. Brigid prayed for her and she was immediately cured.

On that same visit, she met a young boy who was mute and unable to walk. She asked him if he knew where a key was located. "I do," he replied, speaking for the first time. "Then go and get it," she added. He walked and got it.

She could also curb appetites and, by inference, induce weight loss. This is illustrated in the story of Lugaid, a champion boxer, who "had the physical strength of twelve ordinary men" but whose "appetite for food was proportionately excessive."

Lugaid came to her asking that his desire for food be curbed but his strength retained. She gave him her blessing. Afterwards, his appetite was reduced to that of an ordinary man, "while his strength continued equal to the united bodily prowess of twelve labourers."

Given Brigid's intimate association with farming, it was inevitable that some of her miracles would be connected to her line of work. The story is told of how she assembled reapers and labourers to help with the harvest, only for bad weather to intervene. The day was cloudy and wet, and rain poured down from the sky.

Streams overflowed, rivers of water coursed down through the glens, and the surrounding area was flooded. While reapers in nearby farms were hampered by the conditions, Brigid's team worked from dawn to dusk. They never encountered rain, and the harvesting was completed without experiencing problems.

The time-tied character of farmwork – milking the cows, bringing in the cattle, feeding the calves – surfaced in another Brigid miracle. A young girl who visited her found that time had slipped by and evening was fast approaching. "Stay here for the night," Brigid suggested.

The girl pointed out that she had farm duties to attend to at home. "Leave all that to me," Brigid said. The girl decided to stay the night. The following morning, on returning home, she found that all her tasks had been miraculously completed.

Like any farmer, Brigid feared predators and the damage they could do to her stock. One day, a frightened wild boar entered her herd of pigs. The boar was fleeing in terror from some unspecified danger, and the potential for damage was huge. Brigid blessed the boar, whereupon it became calm and submissive. It remained with her from then on.

On another occasion, wild wolves came to her aid and helped guide a gift of "fat pigs" from the plain of the River Barrow to Dunshaughlin, County Meath. It was a three or four-day journey, the narrator recalled. The wolves, out of respect for Brigid, not only rounded up the pigs but drove them part of the way without harming them. What they did was contrary to their nature.

One notable, and controversial, miracle concerned a nun who became pregnant. "Her womb had begun to swell," Cogitosus tells us. Brigid blessed the distraught woman, and with strength of faith ensured that "what had been conceived in the womb disappeared." The outcome was one that would later draw criticism from those with strong views about conception and childbirth.

The following final "miracle" seems more of a good story than a case of divine intervention. The story concerns a fox which was spotted walking near the residence of the king. Thinking the fox was wild and stray, a man passing by killed it. Unfortunately, it was a tame fox and the prized possession of the king.

The king was furious and had the man arrested. He declared, in a passion, that the man be put to death, his wife and children reduced to a state of bondage, and his small property confiscated. Brigid was upset when she heard the news. She prayed to God for help.

She decided to travel to the king and plead for the man's life. On the way, a wild fox approached her wagon from the woods, jumped into it, and settled down in the folds of her clothes. It turned out to be a clever fox, equal in cunning and tricks to the one the king had lost.

She offered a deal to the king: the fox in return for the man's freedom. On seeing how clever the fox was, the king agreed. The man was set free. It seems everyone was happy except the fox. However, he was soon on his way home, having contrived to escape across the countryside despite being pursued by the king's horsemen and dogs.

"All the people, living in that part of the province, admired what had occurred," the Rev. John O'Hanlon wrote in his *Lives of the Irish Saints.* "Her fame was daily on the increase, and she was regarded as the special favourite of Heaven." As a result of these miracles, she also "brought countless souls to the following of Christ," he concluded.

Brigid also secured a miracle for one of her religious companions, Sr. Daria, who was blind. It's a warm and redemptive story with a twist at the end.

One evening, Brigid and Sr. Daria, who had been blind since birth, sat with each other as the sky's brightness dimmed and the sun faded to the west. Most likely they were beginning an all-night vigil on the Curragh downs, watching over and protecting their sheep.

The evening, it seems, was a warm one, probably in the heart of summer. They soon became engaged in conversation. They spoke of the love of Jesus and the joys of Paradise, and their hearts were filled with happy thoughts.

The hours passed by, and the night slid by, too. Neither had noticed the passage of time. Nor had they grown tired or cold; the conversation was that uplifting. Soon, the first morning light appeared, and the sun's rays slowly and gently lit up the sky. A perfect Irish summer's day was beginning.

Brigid marvelled at the distant Wicklow mountains to the east, their western slopes purple-grey in the shadow of the sun rising behind them. The mountains, which gradually took form and shape, melted into a glorious, happy sky.

Closer, the land sparkled in the wonderful sunshine. The fields and trees became radiant in the early-morning light. "The pure white light made the face of earth bright and gay" was how the Rev. Baring-Gould described the scene in his *Lives of the Saints*.

Brigid knew that her blind companion was unable to see the wonderful vista unfolding before her. Her heart sank at the thought of what she was missing. She sighed deeply, upset that Daria, who was known for her holiness, could not experience this early-morning tribute to the glory of God and his creation.

She bowed her head and prayed that her companion might have the faculty of sight given to her and that she might witness all this beauty. "God, please allow Daria to see the loveliness of the earth and sky," she pleaded. She then extended her hand and made the Sign of the Cross on each of her fellow sister's eyes.

Sr. Daria at once gained the gift of sight. She saw perfectly for the first time in her life. "The darkness passed away from them," remarked the Rev. John O'Hanlon regarding Sr. Daria's eyes. She instantly witnessed how "all the trees and flowers glittered with dew in the morning light," he wrote.

She also saw the yellow-pink sunrise peeping over the distant horizon. The clear-blue sky was speckled here and there with puffs of gentle clouds. Far away were the wonderful purple-grey Wicklow hills with their hidden glens, vales and valleys so sweet, "in whose bosom the bright waters meet," as poet and lyricist Thomas Moore would be inspired to write many centuries later.

Sr. Daria looked for a little while, and then, turning to her abbess, said: "Close my eyes again, dear mother, for when the world is so visible to the eyes, God is seen less clearly to the soul." Brigid prayed once more, and Sr. Daria's eyes returned to darkness. She remained blind for the rest of her life.

The Rosary beads as an aid to prayer was said to have been invented by Brigid during her time in Kildare. The claim that she was responsible for its physical form and its use for reciting a pattern of prayers has been made by scholars down through the centuries.

The first knotted rope called the "prayer rope" was devised by an ascetic from Egypt known as Pachomius the Great. With knots tied throughout its length, it was used by the earliest monks to count out prayers. Predating Brigid by about a century and a half, it became a popular method for knowing how many prayers had been said, replacing the early practice of dropping small pebbles into a bowl.

Pachomius set up the first monastic settlement in Egypt, displacing the earlier pattern of monks living solitary lives in huts or caves. Known as Abba by his followers, meaning "father," he is credited with the invention of the title "abbot", which has been used down through the ages. He is also credited with establishing the first written rule for monks.

More importantly, for our purposes, he was aware that his followers, many of whom were illiterate and innumerate, required a method of knowing they were saying the required number of prayers, hence the knotted rope. We can only imagine them, their prayer ropes in their left hands, leaving their right hands free for making the Sign of the Cross, which was already a custom at the time.

Information spread surprisingly quickly. Brigid became familiar with the idea of using a "counter" to mark out the recitation of prayers. She was undoubtedly aware of the use of pebbles; it is equally certain that she knew of prayer ropes. Either way, it is suggested, she fused the two notions together by linking pebbles on a rope and assigning different-sized pebbles to denote the various prayers to be said, such as the Hail Mary and the Our Father.

Her role in inventing what we commonly now refer to as the "Rosary beads" was chronicled by the Irish-born Dominican missionary, preacher and Professor of Theology, the Rev. J. A. Rooney, who was born in the late 1830s, emigrated to America as a young man, and who became an expert on the Rosary. Described as "a logical reasoner and a thorough student," he wrote a scholarly summation of his understanding of what happened in the influential magazine *The Rosary* in 1893.

"She adopted the practice of the anchorites of the East, who had the habit of employing pebbles as counters in their prayers," he wrote. "She wisely judged that it would be more convenient to string together in the form of a crown those very small pebbles, and to designate the different prayers to be recited by the difference in the size of the pebbles. The custom, from being inaugurated in her communities, soon spread everywhere over Ireland. Such was the origin of the chaplet."

Brigid's role in devising the Rosary beads was also chronicled, at an earlier stage, by the eminent French ecclesiastic and scholar, the Abbé de Sambucy, who was born in 1771, and who later compiled the definitive Rosary manual, the *Manuel du Chapelet et du Rosaire*, which was published in 1837. St. Brigid, he wrote, had not only "invented the form" but had "introduced it for pious use to all her monasteries, which caused great excitement."

The later worldwide spread of the Rosary may be attributed to St. Dominic who, as a result of a claimed special revelation from the Virgin Mary, devised the format known to this day.

The Rosary of St. Dominic, who lived from 1170 – 1221, comprised decades of Hail Marys, each of which is preceded by an Our Father. Each decade is also accompanied by meditation on one of the principal mysteries of "the life, sufferings, death, and glory of Jesus Christ, and of His Most Holy Mother."

Through the intense, rhythmic repetition of the main Rosary prayers, allied to the reflective images, it was hoped by Dominic that the mind would become better able to hold on to the truth of the images and gather their full significance. "The recitation became almost a mechanical aid to reflection," one of St. Dominic's biographers, the Rev. Bede Jarrett, explained in 1924. "The thoughts were thereby freer to concentrate, to abstract themselves, to look before and after."

By the time of St. Dominic, the Rosary had come a long way from the primitive construct of Pachomius the Great and the innovative refinements of Brigid of Kildare. In the centuries ahead, it became a centrepiece of Catholic devotion in Ireland. Sodalities, confraternities, church gatherings, prayer meetings based their activities and events around Rosary recitations. Irish people flocked to churches on dark, sombre autumnal evenings and warm summer nights to recite the set of prayers.

The legacy of Brigid's invention reverberated down through the centuries. In Dundalk, during the Eucharistic Congress of 1932, people fell to their knees, clutching their beads while reciting the Rosary at makeshift street altars. Hundreds of thousands did the same in Dublin. In Dunfanaghy, County Donegal, unprecedented numbers arrived for the Rosary at a "beautiful and artistically arranged altar" in the Square. A great number of confraternities gathered to say the Rosary at St. Saviour's Church, Dominick Street, Dublin.

Even St. Brigid might have been shocked by the "Rosary fever" generated during Fr. Peyton's Family Rosary Crusade in 1954. Sixty-thousand people congregated in Waterford to say the prayers; 40,000 did so in Wexford; 30,000 in Galway; 25,000 in Sligo; another 20,000 in Dungarvan; equivalent numbers attended in venues all over the country. Almost all held in their hands a simple set of beads, linked by cord or chain, some in lurid colours, others in dark brown or black, but each apparently owing its genesis to the saint from Kildare.

Brigid's inventive mind also extended to the writing of poetry. A poem attributed to her, *The Heavenly Banquet*, became part of a well-regarded classical song cycle, *Hermit Songs*, composed in 1953 by Samuel Barber.

The idea of a "heavenly banquet" was a metaphor used in the Gospels for the state of supreme, definitive happiness promised to those who reach Heaven. As with any great feast, there was the prospect of good company, rich food and the choicest wines. It was an effective metaphor, used widely in scripture, including by Jesus who compared the Kingdom of Heaven to a wedding feast.

The concept resonated with people who had fewer pleasures in life than are available today. Apart from the joy of listening to music, the prospect of having plentiful food and drink available, without having to struggle to secure them, would bring happiness to people alive at the time of Christ or, later, during the life of Brigid.

The following version of the poem was translated by the 19th-century historian, Professor Eugene O'Curry.

I should like a great lake of ale
For the King of the kings.
I should like the family of Heaven
To be drinking it through time eternal.
I should like the viands
Of belief and pure piety,
I should like flails
Of penance at my house.
I should like the men of Heaven
In my own house;
I should like kieves*
Of peace to be at their disposal.
I should like vessels
Of charity for distribution.
I should like caves
Of mercy for their company.
I should like cheerfulness
To be in their drinking;
I should like Jesus,
Too, to be there (among them).
I should like the three
Marys of illustrious renown;
I should like the people
Of Heaven there from all parts.
I should like that I should be
A rent-payer to the Lord;
That, should I suffer distress,
He would bestow upon me a good blessing.

tubs or vats for holding liquid

The iconic St. Brigid's Cross was also invented by Brigid. She devised it during a visit to a dying pagan chieftain.

Tradition tells us that St. Patrick, on a visit to Meath and nearby counties, used the shamrock to illustrate the doctrine of the Trinity. "How can there be three in one?" a chieftain asked concerning the concept of God as the union of Father, Son and Holy Spirit. Patrick picked up a leaf of shamrock from the ground. "Behold," he said, "three and yet one."

Similarly, Brigid reached for rushes to illustrate another issue of faith. She was visiting a pagan chieftain who lay dying. His servants had summoned her to his bedside in the hope that she might help him as he approached death. She hurried to the dying man, eager to bring him the gift of faith.

Brigid sat by his bed, calming and consoling him, and trying to relieve his distress. He was "raving" and "delirious," it was said. On the floor were rushes, which were commonly used in homes at the time. Their purpose was to keep rooms warm, clean and dry. She looked at them, wondering if they might help her explain the purpose and meaning of Christ's death.

Reaching to the floor, she picked up a handful of rushes and began weaving them into a cross. The sick man watched what she was doing. "What are you making?" he asked. "This is a cross which I make in honour of the Virgin's son, who died for us upon a cross of wood," she replied.

Brigid went on to explain how Christ came to save mankind by his death. Her calming words brought peace to the chieftain's soul. He was so enamoured by what she said that he asked to be baptised. This she did just before his passing, and he died a Christian.

Brigid may have subsequently used her crosses to illustrate points of faith. The truth is, we simply don't know. Somewhere along the way, however, the custom was established for Irish people to fashion St. Brigid's Crosses from straw or rushes and, on the eve of her feast day, to place them inside their houses and byres to ward off illness and disease.

Rushes were also scattered on floors and pathways on the evening before her feast as a form of protection and welcome. As late as the 1960s, in Baile na nGall, County Kerry, people placed them in front of their houses on St. Brigid's night. They did so, too, in the parishes of Rahan, County Offaly, Rathowen, County Westmeath and Greencastle, County Tyrone. The same tradition prevailed in counties Carlow and Kilkenny.

It is unclear how old these traditions are. The first-known record is a manuscript written by the Rev. George Warter Story, who was a chaplain with the Williamite army in Ireland in 1689. He was present at the Battle of the Boyne. As he accompanied the troops during their march to Newry, he noticed that the fleeing Irish left behind houses filled with St. Brigid's Crosses.

"I went abroad into the Countrey, where I found all the Houses deserted for several miles; most of them that I observed, had Crosses on the Inside, above the Doors, upon the Thatch, some made of wood; and others of Straw or Rushes, finely wrought; some Houses had more, and some less," Story noted. Thinking they were charms put up to deter the raiders, the Williamites tore them down.

St. Brigid's Crosses were also worn by Irish knights during the Crusades of the 11th – 13th centuries. Orders of knights who fought under the Christian banner wore various types of crosses on their tunics and shields. To distinguish themselves, the Irish wore the cross of St. Brigid as they rode into battle "for the deliverance of the Holy Land from the infidels."

By the 20th century, the St. Brigid's Cross, along with the shamrock and harp, permeated all corners of Irish life. Telefís Éireann, the Department of Health, the Irish Nursing Board, Irish Girl Guides, schools and sports clubs used her cross as their symbol.

Many rural houses were festooned with St. Brigid's Crosses, which were placed year after year in the attic. The first of them would have been put there by ancestors who had long since passed away. In parts of Kerry, if you counted them you could tell the age of the house.

Brigid's legacy, of course, does not rest on her crosses. Nor does her legacy rest solely on her Irish achievements. Her attention was soon being drawn to the rolling hills and lofty mountains of England and Scotland. In her late 30s, she was heading there over the sparkling, flashing waters of the Irish Sea.

Brigid paid a visit to Glastonbury, South-West England, in 488. Her visit had a long-lasting impact on the area.

Glastonbury, with its sacred monastic settlement, was once one of the great centres of pilgrimage in Europe. The 2,400 religious who lived there carried on the service of God unceasingly day and night. There was the constant sound of hymn singing, with 100 voices chanting hourly, "without rest, without intermission," it was said.

It was a beautiful location to visit. In Brigid's time, it was an island, encircled by water, and covered with fruit trees and shrubs. It was a place where "falls not hail, nor rain, nor any snow, nor ever wind blows loudly," the poet Alfred, Lord Tennyson later wrote. Such was its smiling fertility that it was popularly known as "the happy island."

Her journey to Glastonbury, Somerset, in 488, was far from easy. She first headed south from Kildare, traversing a third of the length of Ireland to Wexford. She then crossed St. George's Channel to Bridgwater Bay near Bristol. From there, she headed to Glastonbury.

It was a well-trodden route, known to numerous Irish pilgrims. St. Patrick, it was said, had traversed it. So, too, did St. Benignus, his successor as Bishop of Armagh. So many Irish pilgrims visited the settlement that it became known as "Glastonbury of the Irish."

Brigid was drawn to Glastonbury not only because it was one of the most important monasteries in Europe, but also because it was a great seat of learning and intellectual power. It was filled with scholars deeply versed in sacred literature. The monks composed and illuminated manuscripts. It was additionally said – correctly, it seems – that King Arthur and his wife Guinevere were buried there. Brigid, in short, was visiting one of the great cradles of Western Christianity.

At Glastonbury, there was contemplation and reflection, scholarly study, singing in wonderful choirs and glorious processions. Importantly, there was prayer. "When all the rest of the world was rocked in slumber, they arose, and flocked in silence to the church, where they remained in prayer and praise until the first faint streaks of dawn began to chase away the constellations of the night," a chronicler of the era wrote of Glastonbury's religious community.

Undoubtedly, Brigid also dispensed spiritual advice and shared practical insights with those she met. Not only was she seasoned and mature at the time of her visit – she was in her late 30s – but her prudence and judgement were highly regarded by her contemporaries. In Ireland, she had interacted with the most eminent persons of her time, including St. Brendan, St. Ailbe and others. She would have continued to do so at Glastonbury.

During her visit, we know that Brigid stayed on the nearby island of Beckery, which housed a colony of monks and maybe even a nunnery. From there, she conducted her evangelical mission, spreading her Christian message and seeking converts to the Church. The island had many Irish connections. Its name is said to have derived from the Irish *Beag Éire*, meaning "Little Ireland." Significantly, following Brigid's visit, Beckery became commonly known as Bride's Hay, Bride's Hill and even Brigid's Island.

Brigid is said to have stayed at a Beckery oratory consecrated in honour of St. Mary Magdalene. She "left there certain signs of her presence – her wallet, collar, bell and weaving implements, which are exhibited and honoured there because of her holy memory," according to *The Chronicle of Glastonbury Abbey*, compiled in the mid-14th century. The bell later disappeared and resulted in an exhaustive search, as we will see further on in this book.

The 14th-century chronicle goes on to state that the chapel on the island "is now dedicated in honour of Saint Bridget," adding that "on its side there is an opening through which, according to the belief of the common folk, anyone who passes will receive forgiveness of all his sins." A nearby spring, known as Bride's Well, was revered for its powers of healing and fertility. In the 1920s, a thorn tree stood there, upon which people would tie rags.

For someone who spent so short a time on her Glastonbury pilgrimage, Brigid certainly left her mark. She was beloved by all who crossed her path. It was no surprise that carvings of her milking a cow would find a place at the church of St. Michael and at the north doorway of St. Joseph's chapel. Pilgrims also later flocked to the area to visit her relics, which were "efficacious in curing divers diseases," according to William of Malmesbury, the 12th-century historian.

Her influence spread far and wide throughout Somerset and beyond. For example, the small coastal village in Pembrokeshire where she is said to have landed is known as St. Brides, overlooks St. Brides Bay, and contains a church dedicated to her name. Fishermen there prayed to her for protection at sea.

Other Somerset villages, towns and even cities also owe a debt to her. Biddisham translates as "Biddy's home." Bittiscombe, Bridgehampton and Bridgetown may have links, too. Even Bristol may be derived from Bride's Stow, meaning "Bride's place." Add in the recognition she receives today in Glastonbury and it is clear that Brigid passed like a whirlwind through the area, leaving an immense legacy in her wake.

Brigid also visited Scotland, where her impact was even greater than at Glastonbury. It was there that the wonderful bird, the oystercatcher, entered her life.

Around the year 500, Brigid headed across the open sea to the cliff-bound shores and purple headlands of Scotland. She landed at a place south-west of Glasgow, which later became known as West Kilbride. It was there – its name a fusion of Bride and *cill* meaning church – that she built her first chapel.

Brigid next built a necklace of small monastic communities along Scotland's south-west coast. Her work – and her fame – soon spread through the country. In time, Scotland was dotted with churches, holy wells and places dedicated to her name, among them 40 Kilbrides and almost 20 Kirkbrides.

It was at one of those Kilbrides, on the island of South Uist in the Outer Hebrides, that oystercatchers entered her life. Legend tells us that these industrious birds, with their straight orange beaks, black-and-white plumage and sturdy pink legs, were the first to greet her when she paid the isle a visit. She was delighted with their welcome.

She came ashore, we are told, with an oystercatcher on each wrist. The legend spread. Soon, locals were calling the oystercatcher *gille Bride*, "servant of Bride." They also called the bird *bridein*, meaning the "bird of Bride." Even more interesting, from our perspective, were the stories told on dark winter nights about Brigid and her beloved birds.

The most important legend describes how, one day, Brigid was pursued along a beach by evil men who wished to kill her. She was alone. Eventually, she became exhausted and collapsed on the sand. There was no place to hide. She prayed to God and thanked him for her life.

Oystercatchers patrolling the shoreline recognised her and hurried to cover her with seaweed. Her pursuers could no longer see her, and her life was saved. As a reward, Brigid blessed the oystercatchers and promised they would rank above all other birds.

Further legends relate to the sea. One story tells how the oystercatcher won favour with Brigid having rescued three motherless infants from a storm. The infants were adrift at sea in a small open boat made of hide. Two oystercatchers, on hearing the children's cries as they flew past, hurried to tell Brigid.

"Saint Bride came immediately to their aid, and guided them on the inflowing tide to a place of safety, where a warm bed of bog-cotton and down had been prepared for them," the Scottish folklorist, Alasdair Alpin MacGregor, wrote in 1924.

Another story told how when Brigid was sailing to Barra, one of the southernmost islands of the Outer Hebrides, she found herself becalmed at sea. Oystercatchers came to her aid. They beat their wings to fill her sails and allowed her to sail her boat to safety.

In thanks, she ensured that while all other birds struggled to make their nests, the oystercatchers would wait until the black mark of the highest tide of the year was seen. They could then build their nests in safety.

Few other saints matched the impact made by Brigid in the Hebrides, or indeed elsewhere in the west or south of Scotland. More churches and chapels were dedicated to her in those regions than to any other saint. Indeed, it is said that the word Hebrides is derived from the phrase "the islands of Bride."

Local fishermen revered her and her sacred birds. At sea they would spot the bird flying overhead, its white breast and wings forming the shape of a cross. The cross, they said, was "given to it by the good St. Bride" as thanks for the many services it provided, including warning them of approaching storms.

Many times, while at sea, they looked at the oystercatcher flying in the sky and saw its white undercoat spread out like the cloak of Brigid. She was there with them, protecting them, helping them, ensuring they were safe, they believed. Nothing could persuade them otherwise.

There were other birds Brigid liked, notably those two heralds of spring, the linnet and the lark. But it was the oystercatcher she liked best. She would listen to them in the evening and smile as they sent their happy call over the waves.

She heard them, too, as she left Scotland to return home to her monastery in Kildare. No doubt, as she set out on her boat, she could hear the birds calling from the shore. "Bi glic!, bi glic!, bi glic!, bi glic!" they chirped, which she, like the Scots, knew from Gaelic to mean "be wise," "be careful," "take care."

And then, when she was gone, they returned to their feeding, their long legs running up and down the edge of the rippling sea. Sometimes, they would rise like a dark cloud against the white of a wave, and the sun would strike its light on the underside of their wings, revealing the cloak of their friend, Brigid of Kildare.

As Brigid approached her 70s, the ravages of age were taking their toll. Knowing that her death was imminent, she held a remarkable conversation with one of her companions.

Four years before her death, Brigid had a revelation that the end of her life was approaching. She initially redoubled her prayers, her fasts and her charitable work. The closer the day came, the greater the amount of time she spent in contemplation of heaven.

She particularly prayed for her religious companions and all those entrusted to her charge. She also took Darlughdach, one of her closest companions, aside and informed her of the precise day and hour of her departure. Darlughdach was distraught and wept bitterly.

Brigid then told Darlughdach that she was to be her successor in charge of the religious houses. Darlughdach was taken aback. How could anyone fill the shoes of such an accomplished holy figure as Brigid? she wondered. In tears, she asked Brigid to relieve her of the burden of authority.

Darlughdach also begged that they should pray together that they might die at the same time. In response, Brigid told her: "My daughter, you will live one whole year after my departure, and then you will follow me." This prediction was fulfilled – both died on 1 February, 12 months apart, and both share the same feast day as a result.

In her final days, Brigid was comforted by the arrival of Ninnid, her priest and confessor, who had rushed from Rome to be by her bedside. When he was a young scholar, she had befriended him having seen him running across a field. "Will you stop and pray with me?" she had asked. "I am running to heaven, which might close if I am not there on time," he had replied.

He did stop that day, and they prayed together. Knowing who she was, he said that her prayers would get him into heaven no matter how late he might be. As a result of their meeting, she would later become the patron saint of students. At one time, she had prophesied that from his hand she would receive the Last Sacraments. That her prophesy was being fulfilled must have brought her great joy.

Old texts indicate that Brigid died on 1 February, in Kildare, somewhere between 523 and 526, at the end of winter and start of spring. It was a time of the year when many old people died, when "the wet and sunless Irish winter has brought vitality low, and the first rifts and gleams in the sky are but a chill promise of spring," as the St. Brigid biographer Hugh de Blacam poignantly put it.

Following her death, sorrow is said to have hung like a pall over Kildare. Her sisters wept. The poor missed her benevolence. Widows and orphans no longer had her protection. Bishops and their clergy had lost a valued mentor. Those who loved and admired her no longer had her to look up to.

They still had her body to venerate, which had been placed in a shrine made of precious metal in her church in Kildare. The shrine, it is said, was beautifully decorated with gold and silver ornaments, and was positioned on one side of the altar. On the other side was buried the body of her old friend, St. Conlaeth, who had predeceased her.

Pilgrims flocked to venerate her remains and seek favours. Yearly the numbers increased. According to the old Kildare monk Cogitosus, many miracles were secured. Unfortunately, to protect her remains from invaders, they had to be removed to Downpatrick for safety. There, as we will see later, they eventually fell into various religious and private hands.

In the meantime, those who venerated Brigid still had her feast day to celebrate. It was a significant date – 1 February – a day of hope, when the border between winter and spring has passed, when darkness turns to light, and when there is everything to hope for and nothing to regret. It was an appropriate date for celebrating the passing of a wonderful woman whose influence would spread down through the centuries.

THE MIDDLE YEARS

Kildare, up to the ninth century, remained a city of great importance, endowed with many ecclesiastical privileges, and regarded as one of the great seats of learning and power.

The finest teachers taught there, and the brightest pupils studied there. Important scholarly works were produced in its halls. The perpetual flame still burned brightly.

Unfortunately, Kildare's days were numbered, and the millennium that followed brought foreign invasions, oppression, famine, emigration and violence.

Through it all, the legend of Brigid flourished. Despite the harsh landscape, her name was revered by many and feared by some, as the following little-known story illustrates all too clearly.

The Anglo-Norman invader "Strongbow" – whose real name was Richard de Clare, 2nd Earl of Pembroke – had a terrifying death. He was haunted by the spectre of St. Brigid as he lay dying in his bed.

In 1176, the Norman warlord Strongbow was dying at his quarters in Dublin. For some time, he had been suffering from an ulcer in his foot. The origin of the ulcer, which was infected, is unclear. It may have resulted from physical combat during his six-year reign of terror in Ireland. It may, perhaps, have been a cancerous tumour.

In his final days, he saw St. Brigid in the act of killing him. She had arrived, according to the *Annals of the Four Masters*, to seek retribution for the many churches in her name that he had desecrated and destroyed. Compiled in the early 1600s, the *Annals* noted that he had also ravaged churches belonging to St. Columcille and other saints. Its authors proposed that these saints combined their efforts to produce the "miracle" of his death.

Strongbow had arrived in Ireland six years earlier, in August 1170, leading an army of 1,200 men, including 200 knights. His aim was to settle territorial disputes and acquire land and titles for himself. Known for his delicate feminine features, bright grey eyes, reddish hair and freckled face, he was a brutal warlord. Battle-hardened from campaigns in Wales, his army of archers and knights landed at Passage East, a fishing village close to Waterford city, on the eve of the feast of St. Bartholomew.

Strongbow and his men were soon breaching the walls of Waterford where they slaughtered people on the streets, hacking them to death without mercy. The gutters in the city's narrow passageways ran red with blood, it was said. They then marched against Dublin, where they repeated the slaughter, brutally murdering those who were unable to escape by boat, and plundering all they could from the terrified inhabitants.

Strongbow next marched on County Meath, where he displayed "a more than ordinary excess of barbarity," it was reported. "Fire, rapine, and murder, everywhere followed in the track of the invaders. Churches and religious houses were burnt down, after being plundered; life was mercilessly sacrificed, without regard to sex or age; and nothing was too sacred or valuable to be for a moment safe from the ravages of the invaders. They returned to Dublin, laden with booty," historian Dr. Samuel Smiles wrote in 1844.

His soldiers were soon invading Wexford, Wicklow and Limerick, where the city was taken and plundered, and a large number of inhabitants slaughtered in cold blood. "Their army was now no better than a mere band of well organised freebooters, who waded to booty through blood, and trampled all honour, honesty, and virtue completely under foot," Dr. Smiles remarked.

They burned down monasteries, plundered churches, and polluted sanctuaries. They particularly ransacked Lismore which, with its college and churches, had long been a renowned seat of literature and religion. The booty was so great that they had to enlist 16 ships to carry the treasures to Waterford. Lismore never recovered its ancient greatness and fell into decay, so great was the damage inflicted.

It was no surprise, then, that Strongbow's death, while in his mid-40s, should have been greeted with immense satisfaction and joy by the Irish. As the *Annals of Inisfallen*, the main record of Munster medieval history, put it, he was the greatest destroyer of the clergy and laity that came to Ireland since the ninth century.

Another set of annals – the *Annals of Tigernach* – concurred, repeating that few brigands "had wrought more ruin than him." The chronicler who wrote that entry had a positive note to end on. "St. Brigid killed him," he concluded, "and he himself used to see her in front of him, killing him." There could be no better retribution than that for Strongbow, one of the most reviled and despised figures in Irish history, he felt.

Three Irish knights are credited with bringing the skull of St. Brigid to Portugal in the late 13th century. The arrival of the relic generated widespread devotion to the saint.

The parish of Lumiar, situated about six miles north of Lisbon, was once a quiet, rural location on the outskirts of one of the oldest cities in the world. Despite being close to Lisbon, it was not the sort of place where you would expect to meet Irish adventurers in the late 13th century. Around 1283, however, three Irish knights arrived, bearing the skull of St. Brigid.

Some suggest the knights stopped off on their way to join the Aragonese Crusade – the Pope's crusade to depose the King of Aragon – but the dates don't appear to fit. Perhaps, instead, they stopped at Lumiar on their way to the Holy Land, hoping to realise their spiritual dream of seeing the Holy Sepulchre or protecting other pilgrims who wished to do so.

No one knows how the knights acquired the skull or why they brought it with them to Portugal. We can, however, deduce how the relic might have come into their hands. We know that, following her death, Brigid was buried in Kildare, where she attracted considerable veneration from pilgrims. Successive attacks by the Danes eventually made the location unsafe and it was thought prudent to move her body to Downpatrick, out of harm's way.

Following further marauding attacks at Downpatrick, the body was at first buried in a secret location and later, in 1186, moved to Downpatrick Cathedral. Eventually, according to the author, the Rev. John J. Gaffney, who wrote the *Life of St.*

Brigid in 1931: "To save these relics during various upheavals, they were divided amongst churches, monasteries, private families and individuals in safer districts." It may well have been as a result of this distributing of her relics that the skull came into the possession of the knights.

The relic ended up in the modestly-sized church of St. John the Baptist in Lumiar, where it remains to this day. The three knights are also buried there. A carving in old Portuguese tells us: "Here in these three sepulchres lie buried the bodies of the three Irish knights who brought the head of the blessed Saint Brigid, a virgin, native of Ireland, whose relic is in this chapel; in memory whereof the officers of the chapel of the blessed saint ordered this to be made in January of 1283."

Down through the centuries, the relic became an object of devotion for people living around Lumiar. In his *Lives of the Irish Saints*, the Rev. John O'Hanlon described how the local farm population – mostly peasant farmers – turned to the relic to protect their animals, replicating a tradition widespread in Ireland. On St. Brigid's feast day, when the relic was exposed, they arrived with their cattle and drove them three times around the church.

Little "leaden oddities" which had touched the relic were then affixed to their horns. "Cows, calves, and oxen, are marched up to the church door, and these little leaden matters, generally a pair of them, are there and then fastened to the horns of the animal and suspended by gay coloured plaited twist, or streamers of ribbons," according to the English author Mrs. Charles Gillingham Hamilton, who witnessed the practice in the mid-19th century.

These traditions came to an end in the early 1930s, due largely to the expansion of Lumiar and its incorporation into metropolitan Lisbon. At around that time – in January 1929 – a portion of the saint's brow was returned to Ireland, where it has rested ever since in St. Brigid's Church, Killester, Dublin. There, it was deposited in a Celtic-designed, silver reliquary and placed in the chapel for all to see.

And so it transpired, by an unusual irony, that a relatively unknown, newly-built suburb of Lisbon handed over a portion of one of St. Brigid's most priceless relics to what was, at the time, a relatively unknown, newly-built suburb of Dublin. From then on, after almost 750 years and a long, hazardous journey, two little churches, located so far apart, have shared this priceless treasure so closely linked to the saint.

St. Brigid's holy well on Clare Island was a popular place of pilgrimage for the famous 16th-century "Pirate Queen" Grace O'Malley, otherwise known as Granuaile.

On a wild, storm-tossed day in 1565, Grace O'Malley, the Pirate Queen, was participating in a pilgrimage at St. Brigid's holy well on Clare Island. Since childhood, she had been visiting this revered well, known as Toberfelabreed, which was set in a bushy hollow, near the beach, on the island's east side. On that day, her prayers and devotions were interrupted when word came that a ship had foundered near Achill Head.

Racing to her boat, she and her companions battled cresting waves, deep troughs and angry seas, and headed to the distant black cliffs of Achill, leaving Toberfelabreed behind them. Disappointment greeted them on arrival as the ship had been broken to pieces on the rocks. Amid the debris, however, a survivor was spotted and brought aboard her boat.

The survivor was Hugh de Lacy, a Wexford man, who Grace brought back with her to Clare Island. There, they began an affair and were eventually "married by the priest of the station, at the altar near the well," it was reported by the 19th-century and early 20th-century antiquarian and folklorist, Thomas Johnson Westropp.

Although, as Westropp explained, they "lived very happily for some years," there was a twist to the story, which we will address later on. Initially, however, it seemed that on that day, St. Brigid's Day, Grace O'Malley had been showered with blessings from above following her visit to the saint's holy well.

It was not surprising that the Pirate Queen had been paying a visit to Toberfelabreed on St. Brigid's Day in 1565. Down through the centuries, her forebears had been deeply immersed in the religious customs and activities of the island, including visits to the holy well. They had also built Clare Island Abbey – officially St. Brigid's Abbey – which they had erected in the late 12th or early 13th century.

It was there, in the abbey, that Grace is believed to have been baptised and buried. Her marriages, apart from the one with Hugh de Lacy, are also said to have been conducted there. The building contains numerous tombs of the O'Malley family along with the O'Malley crest. Together, these features reflect the family's intense Catholicism and devotion to St. Brigid.

Like the O'Malleys, all the islanders, at one time or another, paid homage at St. Brigid's well. Of the two holy wells on the island – the other is dedicated to Mary – Brigid's was by far the most popular. "The patroness that answers by cures must override all rivals," it was noted in deference to the many miracles its waters – unlike the waters of Mary's well – had procured.

The rituals enacted at the well, especially on 15 August, at the height of the harvest, were intricately detailed and a sight to see. Worshippers walked seven times sunward around the outside of the enclosure. This they followed by creeping on their bare knees seven times around the labba – meaning "bed" – and the altar inside the enclosure, emerging at a gap in the north wall. They finished by praying at the well.

The well was credited with many cures, at least two of them being recorded by Thomas Johnson Westropp during several years of research. "We were told how one delicate boy, too feeble to walk without help, was brought by his mother to the place," Westropp wrote. "She put him into the saint's 'labba,' where he fell asleep, while she did the usual rounds, and when she awoke him he was able to walk home with her."

Another cure involved an Irish-American who had returned to Mayo as a result of ill health. "Some time afterwards, hearing so much of the fame of the well on Clare Island, he went thither, stayed for a week, drinking of the well and performing the regular rounds. Finding, after his return home, that his health had permanently improved, he determined on another visit later on, which done, he entirely recovered his health and strength."

The long-term outcome wasn't quite so favourable for Grace O'Malley. Her clan, the O'Malleys, became involved in a feud with the MacMahons of Doona Castle, overlooking Blacksod Bay. The latter ambushed the former during a deer hunt on

Achill Island, and Grace's husband, Hugh de Lacy, was killed during the affray. Grace vowed vengeance, but decided to bide her time.

Eventually, word arrived that the MacMahons were travelling on a pilgrimage to Caher Island, about six miles to the south of Grace's Clare Island base. She and her companions travelled there ahead of them, anchored on the far side of the island, and waited until they landed. She then captured their boats, thereby cutting off their retreat.

After slaying many, she brought the man responsible for killing her husband to Clare Island, where she hanged him along with several of his confederates. She then sailed to the MacMahon stronghold, Doona Castle, surprised the occupants, killed them, and made the castle her chief residence, thus bringing to a vicious and bloody end a sequence of events that had begun on a stormy day, near Achill Head, on the feast of St. Brigid, not many years before.

Ireland's 17th-century nemesis Oliver Cromwell named his first daughter Bridget. In doing so, he set a precedent copied by other members of the Cromwell family.

Bridget Cromwell grew up to be an intense, Bible-loving woman. Not only did she look like her father, think like him, and share his puritanical beliefs, but she also had the dubious distinction of being wife and "first lady" to two Lord Deputies of Ireland who, just like her father, imposed reigns of terror on the Irish population.

No one knows precisely why Cromwell chose the name Bridget for his daughter following her birth in 1624. Perhaps it came from his intense interest in religion and the saints. Maybe it derived from the Irish blood he inherited from Thomas Cromwell, chief minister to King Henry VIII, whose father in turn was fond of Ireland because "his ancestors were born there."

For all his bloodthirsty attributes and later carnage in Ireland, Cromwell was known as a good family man. He fathered nine children, five sons and four daughters, and enjoyed nothing better than spending time in their company. It was said that he would sit by his fireside with his daughter Elizabeth – who he called Betty – on his knee, while Bridget – who he referred to as Biddy – played the harpsichord.

Although Bridget was closest to him in looks and character, his favourite daughter was Elizabeth. She was the apple of his eye. Bridget was reserved and homely, with a long face, long nose, and her father's heavy-lidded eyes. Elizabeth, on the other hand, was attractive, frivolous and flighty. She "acted the part of a princess very naturally," a contemporary noted. In contrast, Bridget's main feature was her piety.

When she was 21 years of age, Bridget married General Henry Ireton, a close friend of her father and a man regarded as her father's "second self." The marriage appealed to Cromwell, who was a great admirer of the general's heroic virtues. Bridget, who "was deeply imbued with her father's opinions," was reported to have readily agreed to the match. Ireton, it was remarked, was influenced by Cromwell's pressure more than "the charms of the lady herself."

Ireton accompanied Cromwell during his Irish campaign, eventually replacing him as military commander. Bridget spent some of that time with him in Ireland, where she acted as "first lady" to her husband, who had been granted the title of Lord Deputy. As a military man, he garnered a dark reputation for the savagery of his methods and his scorched-earth policies. His plan, it was said, was "to finally exterminate by fire and sword the Papal Irishy."

Ireton, following his siege of Limerick, perished from the plague. The "vile body" of this "tall, black thief, with bushy curled hair, meagre, vicious face, sunken, hollow eyes, a complexion between choler and melancholy, a four-square Machiavellian head, and a nose of the fifteens," as one of his detractors described him, was brought home to England and buried in pomp at Westminster Abbey.

Upon Ireton's death, Cromwell fixed upon General Charles Fleetwood to marry his daughter. Like her first husband, he was sent to Ireland as Lord Deputy and to lead the army. Bridget joined him and remained in the country for three years. There, she once again reigned as "first lady." Although it was noted that she provided her new husband with wise counsel in his important role, it was also remarked that she entertained as much contempt for him as she cherished admiration for her first husband.

Fleetwood, too, was a vicious enforcer. He crushed the last remaining resistance to the Cromwellian conquest of Ireland, expropriated Catholic landowners and replaced them with English Protestants, forcibly transported many thousands of Catholics to Barbados, and chaotically attempted to implement a policy of banishing Catholics to the west of the Shannon.

Bridget gave birth to a long line of children with both Ireton and Fleetwood. One of them – Ireton's daughter – was given the name Bridget. Her grandfather, Oliver, adored the child. When she was only six years of age, he would sit her between his knees while discussing affairs of state. Occasionally, someone might object to her presence, but Cromwell would reply: "There is nothing I would discuss with anyone of you which I would not equally confide to that child."

Little Biddy, as she was called, was the essence of discretion. Cromwell often put her fidelity to the test by telling her a secret and then directing her mother and grandmother to try to extract it. No amount of coaxing or threats, or even the prospect of severe punishment, would induce her to reveal the confidential details. She, in turn, adored her grandfather, and her mind, it was said, became a mirror of his own.

Later in life, Biddy became an ardent defender of Oliver's reputation. On one occasion, on a coach journey to London, she overheard a fellow passenger speaking badly of her grandfather. Known for her fiery temper, she berated the passenger for the remainder of the journey. She still hadn't cooled down by the time she arrived in London. On emerging from the coach, she grabbed another passenger's sword from its sheath and challenged the slanderer to fight her on the spot.

This young Bridget, in time, produced yet another Bridget through her marriage to Thomas Bendysh. The family's tradition of employing the name didn't end there. Even in the 19th century, it was still in use. An Emma-Bridget Cromwell entered life in 1816, while a Bridget-Nora Cromwell was born in 1874. In such manner, the name of Ireland's greatest female saint reverberated down through the centuries in the Cromwell family.

As for the original Bridget – Oliver Cromwell's daughter – it was said that the more she aged the more she believed her father's rise to power had been "a special boon from Heaven to a thankless race." It was also reported that, towards the end of her life, she was cheered by the conviction that he had lit a candle in England which would never be extinguished. Those viewpoints mattered little, however, as her death came early, at the relatively young age of 37, and she was buried at St. Anne's Church, in Blackfriars, London.

From as far back as the 17th century, St. Brigid's well at Liscannor, County Clare, has been a popular destination for pilgrims. On the last Saturday in July – the eve of Garland Sunday – Aran Islanders have traditionally flocked there in droves.

The earliest-available records reveal that on the last Saturday in July Aran Islanders have traditionally travelled across six miles of dancing, sparkling water to Doolin in County Clare. On a good summer's day, "the sea shines like a jewel," as songwriter Percy French put it. On a bad day, exposed to an Atlantic swell, the trip can be treacherous.

Each year, they have made the journey to celebrate Garland Sunday at Lahinch, and on the night before to pray and perform the "rounds" at St. Brigid's well in Liscannor. Traditionally, they beached their boats at Doolin and walked the five miles across the cliffs to the holy well. There, a long night of prayer and devotion, intermixed with music and singing, ensued.

"They first perform their rounds, and then spend a good part of the time in invoking this saint Bridget over the well, repeating their prayers and adorations aloud, and holding their conversations with the Saint," the local Anglican clergyman, Archdeacon James Kenny, wrote in 1814. "When this ceremony is over, they amuse themselves until morning by dancing and singing."

The scene at the well was always picturesque. Flickering flames from blazing camp fires cast shadows over kneeling figures as they engaged in prayer. The light revealed singers who sang until dawn. Some of the younger islanders danced; others quietly slipped off to nearby taverns. Locals, drawn by the extraordinary spectacle, sat at a distance, watching the night's proceedings unfold.

The islanders were drawn by an age-old belief that St. Brigid had stopped at the spot on her way to Munster. She had rested where the well now sits. An extended version of the legend says that during her stopover she had preached to a big congregation. When departing, the well sprang up on the spot where she stood. Tradition also claims that she left an eel in the well which, if spotted, guaranteed that the person seeing it would have his or her wish granted.

Many miracles and cures were reported following visits to the well, including revivals from eye problems, rheumatism, ulcers, headache, and that recurring ailment of the time – toothache. Perhaps the best-known cure was experienced by the local landowner Cornelius O'Brien – an MP who, Lord Palmerston once said, was "the best Member Ireland ever sent to Westminster, for he was in the House thirty years and never once opened his mouth."

At one time, O'Brien lay ill in London, where several doctors despaired of his condition and feared he might die. He asked for water to be procured from the well at Liscannor, and it was sent to him in London. It "at once restored him to health," reports said. In thanksgiving, he renovated the well. He even hired a piper to entertain visitors at the nearby Cliffs of Moher. Unfortunately, the piper fell over the cliffs while drunk!

Another miracle at the well was recorded by Lady Gregory and was published in 1908. "I brought my little girl that was not four years old to Saint Brigit's well on the cliffs, where she was ailing and pining away," a woman told her. "I brought her as far as the doctors in Gort and they could do nothing for her and then I promised to go to Saint Brigit's well.

"From the time I made that promise she got better. And I saw the little fish when I brought her there; and she grew to be as strong a girl as ever went to America. I made a promise to go to the well every year after that, and so I do, of a Garlic Sunday, that is the last Sunday in July. And I brought a bottle of water from it last year and it is as cold as amber yet."

The "Garlic Sunday" referred to by that woman was another name for Garland Sunday, which was popularly celebrated at the time. The name derives from the festival's connection with flowers. Lady Wilde described how garlands of flowers were decorated the night before with coloured ribbons, and only single girls were allowed gather the flowers and wreathe the decorations, for "the touch of a married woman's hand in the decorations was deemed unlucky."

Garland Sunday was, and still is, held on the last Sunday in July and once attracted huge crowds to Lahinch. Although other, newly-arrived pilgrims would attend St. Brigid's well at Liscannor on that day, the Aran Islanders would depart and walk four miles to Lahinch for a carefree day of fun by the sea.

"It was a real day of sport there on the strand," Clareman Seán Mac Mathúna, a contributor to the records of the Irish Folklore Commission, remarked in 1942. "In the old days there used to be a horse-race on the sand and crowds of people watching it. In the town itself and on the Promenade there were crowds to be seen, and every one seeking some kind of sport. There used to be the whole world of tricksters there, each trickster of them making as much noise as if he were paid for it.

"The man of the musical instrument was there and the dancing woman, the card-man, and the man that used to frighten us when we watched him dipping a fork in the barrel of blazing tow and putting it into his mouth and down into his throat. And if the tinkers were not there with their women and children it is not yet a day!"

Unfortunately, Garland Sunday sometimes degenerated into drinking and violence, not by any means the fault of the islanders. It was a day, one newspaper said, of "faction-fighting and scenes of disorder, mingled with revelry and boisterous enjoyment." The pubs were packed, alcohol was drunk, a few "made a show of themselves," blows were struck, and recriminations followed.

In 1938, the Guards were attacked. They were forced to launch a baton charge against a crowd of 200 men. Seven young men appeared in court. "I was all black and blue next morning. The kicks ranged from my ankles to my hips," one Guard explained. On adjourning the case for 12 months, the judge remarked to the accused: "If any of you appear before me after next Garland Sunday, then God help you!"

The festival was also an occasion for bachelors to obtain a bride by lottery. Prospective wives took part in a parade while sitting in painted ass-drawn carts. Gaping prospective husbands eyed them closely. The ladies' names were then placed in a tin can; the names of the men were placed in another.

Great excitement followed as names were drawn and couples matched. "Each draw brought ringing cheers from the onlookers and if the 'husband' had secured a good 'catch' he immediately made tracks to the nearest pub to celebrate his good fortune with his friends," according to a newspaper report from as late as the mid-20th century.

We don't know if any wives were secured by the islanders at Lahinch, but we do know that the weekend was regarded as one of the most treasured times in their year. They left exhausted yet invigorated, and headed out into an ocean overshadowed by the Cliffs of Moher boldly standing like ramparts against the might of the sea.

As they left, they were waved at and bade farewell by the local inhabitants, who gathered on the shore. "God speed," they shouted after them, "Safe home. We will see you same time next year."

St. Brigid's well, at Cormakilly, County Donegal, close to the border with County Tyrone, became a focal point for illegal Masses during the persecution of Catholics under the 18th-century Penal Laws.

At the end of a narrow glen, in a setting of hazel and hawthorn trees, St. Brigid's well at Cormakilly seemed a safe, secluded place to hold a secret Mass. It was there during the time of the Penal Laws that a visiting priest, Fr. James Gallagher, was illegally, and perilously, ministering to the spiritual needs of the local population.

During the course of the Mass, the enemy was sighted. Fr. Gallagher threw the altar candles into St. Brigid's well, took to his heels, and fled up the nearby slope. With his enemy in pursuit, he ran towards the house where he had been lodging. His congregation, who were themselves fleeing in panic, never saw him again. He was believed to have been killed and his body disposed of.

He wasn't the only priest in the area who was hunted down like a dog. Another priest, Fr. Mac a Ward, who lived just across the border in County Tyrone, was tracked to his little house one bright moonlit night. It was "a grand night for a hunt, and a right long one it was," it was remarked. The priest ran for his life, three miles up a long hill, being relentlessly pursued. He reached the top of the hill, where he fell exhausted.

There, his enemies overtook him and killed him. It was said that they cut off his head. By the time his parishioners arrived, it was all over. They placed his mangled body on a hastily put together litter, and with hand-spokes made of willow, carried his body back towards his makeshift altar. Terrified of being seen, they changed their minds and buried him in the moss. It is believed that two willow trees, grown from the hand-spokes, mark his grave to this day.

The Penal Laws of the 18th century struck terror in the Catholic population not only of counties Donegal and Tyrone but of the whole island of Ireland. Masses were banned, priests imprisoned, exiled or killed. In 1709, the Irish Parliament passed a resolution declaring it "an honourable act" to inform against the clergy. A reward of £50 was voted for the discovery of a bishop; £20 for the arrest of a clergyman. Priest-hunters roamed the land.

Priests went on the run and held Masses in hidden valleys, open fields, garrets of ruined buildings, and in secret houses. They celebrated their Masses at rocks or at isolated holy wells like St. Brigid's in Cormakilly. There, among tokens of favours received or favours expected, they spread out their chalices, candles and patens, and placed their hope in God that they wouldn't be betrayed and killed.

There was nowhere safer to hold a Mass, it seemed, than at St. Brigid's holy well in Cormakilly. Situated close to the border between counties Donegal and Tyrone, near Castlefinn and Clady, the isolated townland was believed, at the time, to be safe from priest-hunters. Sparsely populated, the area was better known for its jagged blue thistles, scent of wild privets, and yellow-breasts arguing with the wind, than for any human intrusions.

Set in the heart of the Finn Valley, the well in honour of St. Brigid was regarded as so sacred that people paying visits would never touch the dense weeds growing nearby. It attracted a constant stream of pilgrims, who left locks of hair and other tokens in gratitude for miracles hoped for or received. Unfortunately, it became a place where "the blood of priest and people was poured out with the chalice of Our Lord," according to the Donegal parish priest, Fr. Walter Hegarty, speaking in the 1940s.

The killing fields of Donegal yielded a rich harvest. In 1743, Dr. James Gallagher, Bishop of Raphoe, paid a secret visit to the north of the county, where he stayed with a Fr. O'Hegarty at his home on the banks of Lough Swilly. Word got out that he was there. One night, when unable to sleep, the bishop felt an urge to flee elsewhere. Before sunrise, he was on his way to Rathmullan.

As the sun rose, a troop of military was seen hastening from Milford. They surrounded Fr. O'Hegarty's house and shouted: "Out with the Popish Bishop!" They were enraged when the priest informed them that the bishop had been there but was gone. Instead, they arrested the aged cleric, tied his hands behind his back, and carried him off as a prisoner. When locals intervened along the route, the military shot the priest dead and dumped his body on the roadside.

Dr. John McColgan, Bishop of Derry, was luckier. He was also forced to take refuge in Donegal. He did so in his native mountains of Carndonagh, in Inishowen. One evening, the man he was staying with – a Presbyterian farmer – got news that a hunting party was on its way to his home. He saddled two horses and the pair sped to Lenankeel, where the bishop was put aboard a boat to Fanad. Unfortunately, worn out by fatigue and anxiety, he died soon after.

In the 1930s, St. Brigid's holy well at Cormakilly – the scene of so much tragedy during the era of the Penal Laws – was upgraded by workers from in and around Clady, the nearby village, situated just across the border in County Tyrone. They fashioned a grotto near the well and placed there a statue of the saint.

People travelled to the upgraded well in large numbers, although the cattle which once drank its waters were now banned from doing so by a newly-built circular wall. "Wiser people," one cynic remarked, had found the place so sacred that they decided it must be "brought up to date."

St. Brigid's well, however, still remembered its past. Below the grotto, in black letters on a white slab, a simple inscription recalled: "Father James Gallagher said his last Mass at Tobar Brigde in Penal Times." It was a lasting tribute to a grim era when "the heads of priests were bought for a few pounds," according to a remark in the old *Irish Weekly*.

St. Bride's Church, located on Fleet Street, London, is often referred to as "the journalists' church." Named after the Irish saint, its steeple is famous for inspiring the first tiered wedding cake, which was made in the late 18th century.

In 1767, a 12-year-old boy named William Rich travelled to London from the tiny village of Long Newnton, on the border between Gloucestershire and Wiltshire. His plan was to become an apprentice pastry cook in the city. It was a long journey – 100 miles – for the young lad to make, but it turned out to be well worth it.

Records from the era show that William signed on with William Stiles, a cook, for a seven-year apprenticeship. Later, he set up his own business, married, raised a large family, and went on to financial success. Along the way, he also invented the first tiered wedding cake, with each layer diminishing in size from bottom to top. It was a landmark moment, inspiring millions of similar cakes in the centuries ahead.

William's invention came to life in a simple and romantic way. Smitten by a young lady named Susannah Prichard, the daughter of a wig-maker, he courted her and eventually asked for her hand in marriage. The wedding was arranged for 1776, two years after he had finished his apprenticeship. Wishing to do something special for the occasion, he received inspiration from an unlikely source.

Walking along Fleet Street, he happened to notice St. Bride's Church, whose multi-layered steeple was described by the 19th-century historian John Heneage Jesse as one of the most beautiful in London. Designed and built by architect Christopher Wren, it boasted – and still boasts – a series of layers looking exactly like a wedding cake! Back then, however, the concept of such a cake didn't exist.

William decided to model his cake on the steeple of St. Bride's. It wasn't an easy task. Up to then, savoury pies along with single-tiered rich fruit cakes and pound cakes were standard fare at weddings. The pound cakes might be iced, with white icing normally chosen to signify purity and virginity. How to create an iced multi-tiered cake without causing it to collapse was a different matter. He succeeded, and a new wedding rage was born.

At the time when William Rich was being inspired by Fleet Street's famous church, the thoroughfare was already a bustling centre of activity for the newspaper, publishing and printing trades. William Caxton's apprentice, Wynkyn de Worde, had set up a first printing shop there around 1500. *The Daily Courant* – Britain's first daily newspaper – arrived in 1702. A long line of other enterprises followed, bringing worldwide fame to the street.

Alongside the bustle of the print and publishing industries was a building that would fast become known as "the journalists' church." St. Bride's, as it was called, stands on a site where the Romans erected a temple shortly after their invasion of Britain in 43 AD. Six centuries later, a new church dedicated to Ireland's St. Brigid was built on the same site. Ideally located, it was always of importance, with King John holding a parliament within its walls in 1210.

It was, however, the arrival and expansion of the press that propelled the church to its renowned status. By the late 19th century, more than 130 daily and weekly newspapers, along with general literature publishers, operated on Fleet Street, providing reading material "for the education and amusement of the community at large," as one commentator put it. Their local church was St. Bride's.

Journalists, columnists, editors, printers and office staff from a long line of titles – *Daily Telegraph*, *Daily Express*, *Daily Mail*, *Daily Mirror*, *Financial Times*, among numerous others – walked through its doors on a regular basis. The church provided a tranquil respite for employees of these establishments. It had "a peaceful, old-world aspect, which is delightfully soothing when one passes from the turmoil of Fleet Street into the quietude of the sacred building," as A. E. Daniell put it in *London City Churches*, published in 1896.

Although by the end of the 20th century the great days of Fleet Street were over, St. Bride's never lost its newspaper connections. In 1998, the funeral of Lord Rothermere, proprietor of the *Daily Mail*, *Mail on Sunday* and *London Evening Standard*, was held there. In 2016, the church hosted the wedding of model Jerry Hall and media mogul Rupert Murdoch. On ordinary weekdays, however, hollow echoes resonated through its pews and aisles.

"Every few months I have lunch with two friends in the shadow of the journalists' church of St. Bride's in Fleet Street, London," wrote Harry Eyres, in 2013, in the *Financial Times*. "One gets a certain melancholy frisson walking down the former main drag of English journalism, past the splendid art deco buildings that once clanked and thrummed as printers, typesetters and journalists worked on different floors – headquarters of newspapers that have either upped sticks to more anonymous offices or disappeared altogether."

Although the print media had departed, William Rich hadn't left with them. After going on to success as a cook and "venison dealer" – and having lived at nearby Ludgate Hill with his wife, Susannah, with whom he had 12 children, although five had died at or shortly after birth – he passed away in 1811, at the age of 56, and was buried at St. Bride's.

His wife, Susannah, who had died a year before him, was buried at St. Bride's, too. Throughout their lives they had retained links with the church. Today, however, if they were alive, they might smile at how they are remembered, not necessarily as good parishioners but as the couple linked to what many tourists now refer to as Fleet Street's "wedding cake church."

St. Brigid's convents were suppressed and disbanded during the 16th-century Reformation and Dissolution of the Monasteries. To everyone's surprise, they rose again in 1807 and are still in operation today.

On 1 February 1807, the feast day of St. Brigid, the Order of Brigidines, or Sisters of St. Brigid, came back into existence after being suppressed for almost three centuries. That morning, a small group of nuns assembled in their new convent at Tullow, County Carlow, having spent the previous evening in humble and earnest prayer.

The nuns, ranging from 25 – 48 years in age, included the appropriately-named Bridget Brien; the others were Eleanor Tallon, Judith Whelan, Margaret Kinsella, Eleanor Dawson and Catherine Doyle. All were natives of Tullow and the surrounding parishes of Ardattin and Clonmore. That day, they were dedicating themselves to a life of poverty and chastity, and to God.

Their founder, Bishop Daniel Delany, had set for them a tough way of life. They rose at five o'clock each morning, and a full hour was spent in prayer before Mass. Silence was observed at stated times of the day. Meat was served twice a week, and there was no tea, save on special occasions. It was, the bishop said, "hard living," with "perfect obedience," fasting and "constant application to work and prayer."

Their dress code was practical, yet partly reflected the style chosen by St. Brigid. Their everyday habit of black material with white cap was not unlike the outfit worn by Presentation nuns. On the other hand, following Brigid, they wore entirely white dress when taking part in processions of the Blessed

Sacrament and on feasts of the Blessed Virgin, St. Brigid's Day, Easter, Pentecost and Christmas.

Their work entailed educating the young, both rich and poor alike. With this in mind, they opened a school for the children of the parish and were soon building accommodation for boarders who previously were obliged to stay in town. They then spread farther afield – to Mountrath, Abbeyleix, Goresbridge, Paulstown and Ballyroan. The seed sown by Bishop Delany was fast growing into a tree.

That allusion to a seed-inspired tree is appropriate, as Bishop Delany had brought a tiny oak sapling from Kildare and planted it in the grounds at Tullow during the convent's early days. The sapling was a symbol representing continuity from the convents of St. Brigid to their reinstatement centuries later. Like Bishop Delany's sapling, the order was growing and flourishing.

Delany was an exceptional man. During the time of the Penal Laws, when only Protestant schools were lawful and Catholic schools were banned, he daily set out to pursue an education at a hedge school. He soon revealed himself to be a boy of uncommon quickness. His brilliance brought him to France, where he continued his education and ended up being ordained a priest.

On his return to Ireland, in his 30th year, he was appalled by the conditions that prevailed in the country. The poverty, crime, lawlessness, despair and poor education standards were beyond anything he had witnessed abroad. He started a choir, a band, a Sunday School, and he was soon transforming the parish of Tullow where he was based. After being appointed Bishop of Kildare and Leighlin in 1788, he wanted more, which is when he was struck by the idea of re-forming the order of St. Brigid.

Bishop Delany died in 1814, but his order lived on and thrived. In 1883, the Brigidines received a call from Australia where urgent education needs had arisen. They answered the cry for help, and six sisters were assigned to travel there. They did so aboard the *Chimborazo*, a part steam and part sail-driven vessel, which normally ferried over 100 passengers along with cargo, often including sheep on the foredeck, to the "Land of the Southern Cross."

The sisters knew they were unlikely to see Ireland again. "We came on board the *Chimborazo* at about 10 o'clock pm – never felt so lonely in all my life.....the bell rang at 2.00 am to warn visitors to leave the ship; it was then indeed my heart sank. Fr. Phelan wasn't able to speak to us he could not conceal the tears that welled up in his eyes.....We went to our cabins and had a nice cry. We dined at six and indeed mingled tears with our dinner," one of the pioneering women wrote in her diary.

The conditions in Australia were far from ideal. Financial difficulties, a merciless climate and violent epidemics made the nuns' path a thorny one. On one occasion, a typhoid epidemic caused the indefinite closure of one of their schools. The prolonged drought of another year almost destroyed the sheep-farming industry on which the wealth of the colonists – and the finances of the order – depended. Yet the sisters survived and their activities flourished.

Throughout the late 1800s, the Brigidines carried the name and legend of St. Brigid through the broad expanse of Australia.

They were soon operating in Victoria, Queensland, New South Wales, and Western Australia. They also crossed the Tasman Sea to New Zealand. They were still, of course, operating in Ireland.

They had travelled a long way from home, yet by the standards of St. Brigid, there was no surprise in that. She, too, had journeyed to the distant lands of her time, and her convents had spread far and wide. Her successors were no different. And wherever they went, they customarily planted an oak sapling in honour of their patron, St. Brigid of Kildare.

The Irish nationalist Michael Cavanagh, who fought in the 1848 Young Ireland rebellion, had a translation of an ancient hymn to St. Brigid published in the American and Irish press. An excerpt is reproduced below.

Michael Cavanagh, from Cappoquin, County Waterford, was in his mid-20s when he took part in the unsuccessful Young Ireland rebellion of 1848. The following year, he was involved in an assault on his local police barracks, during which a constable and one attacker were killed. Later that year, he decided to leave for America, where he arrived in January 1850.

In New York, he was active in the Fenian Brotherhood and continued as a member until 1866. Eventually, he moved to Washington D.C., where he worked at the War Department and flourished as a writer. His numerous works were published in newspapers, magazines and books, winning him widespread praise.

On 1 February 1882 – St. Brigid's Day – he translated part of an ancient hymn in praise of St. Brigid, which is contained in the *Liber Hymnorum*, held by Trinity College, Dublin. We saw a reference to that hymn earlier in this book regarding St. Brendan's visit to Brigid.

As pointed out then, the hymn may have had any of a number of composers, but Cavanagh attributes it to St. Columcille. It might equally have been composed by St. Brendan, St. Ultan or St. Broccan Cloen. Cavanagh's translation was originally published in *The Boston Pilot*, and later in *The Dundalk Democrat*.

COLUMKILLE'S INVOCATION TO ST. BRIDGET

St. Bridget! virgin pure and bright,
Our sun by day our torch by night;
St. Bridget radiant, though unseen,
The handmaid meet of Heaven's Queen!
Oh! may St. Bridget guard us well,
From all the fiendish host of hell,
And may she smooth our pain through life
While in this weary world of strife;
Oh! may this brand of God's own fire,
Expel from us each low desire.
Yes, she shall aye our safeguard be,
Dear Saint of Leinster, fair and free;
Next holy Patrick she shall stand,
The prop and stay of Erin's land;
Resplendent midst the saints serene,
Among all queens she shines a queen.
When age shall lay our follies bare,
Be Bridget's grace like shirt of hair –
To bring repentence to the soul.
May Bridget guard us to the goal!

New York's St. Brigid's church, which was constructed in the late 1840s by Irish immigrants, became famous during the American Civil War. Its pastor, Fr. Thomas Mooney, became well known for his part in the conflict. Its parishioners also fought in many of its battles.

The men of New York's 69th Infantry Regiment had one of those spine-tingling moments on the afternoon of 23 April 1861. One thousand of them – led by Sligo-born Colonel Michael Corcoran – had assembled at Great Jones Street, where they were presented with a United States flag by the wife of Galway-connected Judge Charles Patrick Daly. Ordered to march at three o'clock, they never anticipated what was about to happen next.

The men of the "Fighting 69th", as they were called, turned on to Broadway as they headed towards the New York piers and their departure for the Civil War. As they entered Broadway, they were greeted by a tumultuous farewell. The street was crammed with well-wishers. The cheers were deafening. Flags and banners streamed from windows and housetops. Ladies waved their handkerchiefs from balconies and flung bouquets on the marching column.

Soaking up the atmosphere was the regiment's chaplain, Fr. Thomas Mooney, who was the pastor of New York's recently-built St. Brigid's church. A Manchester-born immigrant of Irish parentage, he felt at home with his fellow recruits, many of whom were his parishioners. Since 1853, he had been priest-in-charge at St. Brigid's – a church which, it was said, was "worthy of so great a saint."

Many of Fr. Mooney's army colleagues and parishioners who marched with him that day had arrived in America having escaped the Great Famine in Ireland. They had names like Duffy, Murphy, Kelly, Butler, O'Boyle, Cahill and Ryan. Their paymaster was Matthew Kehoe. Two of their assistant surgeons were named Kiernan and Nolan. All of them were part of a military unit that would rightly and understandably be called the "Irish Brigade".

No other Union company suffered more combat deaths than the Irish Brigade during America's Civil War. Inspired by their battle cry "Faugh a Ballagh" – an anglicisation of "Fág an Bealach," meaning "clear the way" – they fearlessly engaged their Confederate counterparts in close, deadly combat. They became known for their courage, ferocity and toughness in battle, resulting, of course, in disproportionate fatalities.

Few members of the brigade were more courageous than Fr. Mooney. He never lacked energy or spirit, and was daring and tenacious. Wherever his fellow recruits went, he went, too. He said daily Masses for the troops and heard their Confessions. A kind and considerate man, he also offered counsel to soldiers who faced death on a daily basis.

The men of the 69th loved him. Those who knew him from St. Brigid's recalled "a friend to whom they could always come with confidence," as one sketch from the era put it. Many of them were hardened Irish immigrants, who had worked on the New York docks in backbreaking labour. It was their rough hands that had built St. Brigid's, turning it into a haven for themselves and their families. They knew a trustworthy, sincere man when they met one.

They also recognised and appreciated the priest's wild Irish streak. On one occasion, he was asked to bless a cannon gun, but he decided to baptise it instead. It was an honour throughout his time as a priest, he jokingly said, "to baptise many a fine blue-eyed babe, but never had I brought before me such a quiet, healthy, and promising fellow as the one now before me."

His boss, Tyrone-born Archbishop John Hughes – known as "Dagger John" for his abrasive personality – wasn't amused. He immediately sent Mooney a letter: "Your inauguration of a ceremony unknown to the Church, viz., the blessing of a cannon was sufficiently bad, but your remarks on that occasion are infinitely worse. Under the circumstances, and for other reasons, I wish you to return, within three days from the receipt of this letter, to your pastoral duties at St. Brigid's."

Fr. Mooney was left with no choice. Against the wishes of his comrades, he returned to New York, where a surprise awaited him. Four thousand parishioners turned out to greet him and welcome him home. He was so popular that when the "Fighting 69th" later returned to the city, they asked him to lead their parade. He was only too happy to oblige.

For the next decade and a half, Fr. Mooney attended to his pastoral work at St. Brigid's. Then, in 1877, aged 53, he was involved in a dreadful accident. He was thrown from his carriage while driving through Fifth Avenue, the vehicle having hit a heap of stones which had been left unlit and unguarded. Thrown violently against the kerbstone, his skull was fractured. Although there were hopes of a recovery, he died a few days later, on 13 September 1877.

His funeral service, which was held at St. Brigid's, was memorable. Outside the church, an estimated 10,000 people crammed the streets. One hundred policemen struggled to keep them under control. The church itself was packed to capacity. Six bishops and 400 priests sat with his regular parishioners. "As the solemn service echoed through the aisles of the mourning church, the sobs of the humble parishioners became uncontrollable," one newspaper reported.

The sombre occasion was marked by another sound that left an indelible imprint on those in attendance. It was the sad, muffled roll of the drum corps of the "Fighting 69th". Along with large detachments of the regiment, they had arrived to pay their respects to one of their fallen dead. It was their final tribute – their last tattoo – to a man who had marched with them from St. Brigid's church in New York to some of the most vicious battlefields of the American Civil War.

St. Brigid's Orphanage, Eccles Street, Dublin, was an innovative institution catering for the orphan children of the Catholic poor. Established in 1857 by the Waterford-born Margaret Aylward, it was operated under the patronage of St. Brigid.

There was open warfare on the streets of mid-19th-century Dublin as two warring factions – one Protestant, the other Catholic – fought to save the souls of the children of the poor. The Protestant faction was led by a formidable woman, of deep religious conviction, named Ellen Smyly. Her Catholic adversary, Margaret Aylward, was an equally-formidable woman who held passionate religious beliefs.

In an effort to save orphans from the clutches of Smyly's proselytisers, Aylward fought what could only be called a "holy war." She and her companions paid visits to Smyly's Protestant orphanages and schools to identify Catholic children induced there by offers of food and clothing. Loud arguments erupted. Scuffles took place. Battles spilled onto the streets. Crowds of agitated bystanders often assembled, adding to the mayhem.

In order to save these poverty-stricken "little ones" from Smyly's dens of "heresy and perdition," as Aylward described them, a decision was made in 1856 to establish an orphanage to cater for the Catholic poor. Inspired by a vision of St. Brigid which Aylward's spiritual advisor, Fr. John Gowan, had as a child, the proposed orphanage was placed under the saint's protection. It was formally opened in 1857.

The new orphanage was both cost-efficient and innovative. In contrast to the prevailing system of housing orphans in expensive centralised institutions, St. Brigid's placed its children with approved Catholic families. Farmers located in counties close to Dublin were chosen, each of them being paid an annual fee in return for giving shelter to a child.

Education, clothing and religious instruction were provided by the families. In return, the children contributed to farm work. The hope was that, alongside other children in the family, they would "eat at the same table, play together, are clothed alike, call their nurses 'mother' and enjoy a mother's affection," according to the orphanage's first annual report. To ensure this objective was being met, regular inspections and surprise visits were undertaken.

From its inception, St. Brigid's began the process of boarding out thousands of children saved from "orphanages of error, foundling hospitals, charter schools, military schools, almshouses, and receptacles of heresy," as Aylward put it. Forty-three children were taken in during its first year in operation; the number rose to 103 in the second year; and by 1907 a remarkable 3,500 homeless children had been provided for.

"The mode of management of this institution is almost unique," the English-born author Fanny Taylor, who visited the orphanage in the mid-1860s, commented. "The children of St. Brigid are placed with respectable peasants in the country, who are paid for each child's board and clothing. These families are carefully selected, and are bound by certain rules in regard to the children, such as that they shall be kept clean and tidy and sent to school.

"At certain times the managers of St. Brigid's go to the place where the orphans are and hold an examination, and prizes are given to the parents, consisting of ten shillings for each child that proves to have been kept up to the standard which the managers have laid down for it. The plan has answered admirably; the work of St. Brigid's has been visibly blessed."

In the main, St. Brigid's brought happy outcomes for the orphans. One little boy showed his gratitude by presenting the sisters with his Christmas box of four shillings. Another boy, after being granted a rise in wages, said to them that not only could he now support his "poor mother" but he would "pay for two of the orphans, too."

Yet another boy, who had learning difficulties, was adopted by a nurse when she heard that the institution could no longer keep him and he would have to be sent elsewhere. "He is a loving child," she said, "and if he must be put off the books, I'll keep him. I'll be a mother to him."

Contrary to these good-news stories, the centre courted controversy in 1858 over a case involving an orphan named Mary Mathews. The child had been brought there after her father, who was caring for her, died. Her mother had earlier moved to the West Indies to work. On her return, the mother discovered the fate of her daughter and demanded that she be returned to her care. As the orphanage had already fostered out the child, this was refused.

The matter ended up in court, where Aylward was given a six-month sentence for contempt of court for not producing the child. Public controversy ensued. "We cannot but heartily approve of this verdict, and we believe it will give very general satisfaction," the Protestant-oriented *Kerry Evening Post* declared. The Catholic-owned *Tuam Herald* thoroughly disagreed. "The case of Miss Margaret Aylward cannot fail to elicit the deepest sympathy of the entire Catholic community," one of its editorials proclaimed.

As the controversy raged, Aylward served her full six-month sentence in harsh conditions in Dublin's Grangegorman female penitentiary. Although she emerged in poor health, she returned with vigour to her work. She was soon establishing a range of schools under the patronage of St. Brigid – the first in Dublin's Crow Street, the second in Great Strand Street, followed by two more in West Park Street, the latter being located "just opposite the great proselytising school on the Coombe."

Along with her St. Brigid's schools, Aylward additionally set up the congregation known as the Holy Faith Sisters, which remains active to this day. By 1909, its 14 convents were providing for an estimated 7,000 children, not only educating them in primary schools, private day schools, infants' schools and junior boys' schools, but often providing pupils with clothes and daily breakfasts.

Side by side with this remarkable work, Aylward remained committed to her orphanage up to her death in 1889. More than a century after its inauguration, it was still operating at its Eccles Street premises. It only moved from there in the 1970s, first to Iona Road and then to the Coombe, bringing to an end "a simple story of a good work silently, laboriously, and successfully carried on," as author Fanny Taylor concluded after her visit to it in the 1860s.

The Nun of Kenmare, who was an admirer of St. Brigid, was one of the best-known Irish women in the second half of the 19th century. She was highly praised for her work during the famine of 1879.

Margaret Anna Cusack – otherwise known as the Nun of Kenmare – was regarded as the most famous Irish lady of her day and the most famous Irish nun since the time of St. Brigid. She was a bestselling author, admired by the Pope, loved by the poor, founded her own order, and was a thorn in the side of Irish landlords and senior clergy.

A Dubliner by birth, she became an Anglican nun but eventually left and converted to Catholicism. After joining the Poor Clares in Newry, she was sent in 1861 to help found the

Convent of Kenmare, County Kerry. For the next two decades, she made the town internationally famous through her numerous books, including her *Life of St. Brigit*.

Kenmare was "a lovely village, three hours' drive from Killarney" and known for "the beauty of its scenery," she noted in her autobiography. The Elizabethan-style convent, adjoining the church, stood in a large and beautiful garden, and was set in "the most beautiful parish of the most beautiful county of the south of Ireland," an American journalist, who visited her in 1880, remarked.

The journalist, James Redpath, provided his readers with a rare insight to her looks and demeanour. She was, he said, "a little woman, with delicate and refined features, and a pale and sweet face, with signs of the weariness that physical suffering leaves behind it, but without a single trace of badness; yet a face that would have looked sad but for the merry beaming of her bright and keen brown eyes." Like the Abbess of Kildare, she was, he commented, "generous," "sincere" and "cordial."

Known far and wide as the Nun of Kenmare, she helped put into practice the devotional traditions devised by her role model, St. Brigid. "We have our special devotions for Christmas and Lent, for the sorrows of the Passion and the joys of Easter, and what helps us now heavenward, helped our ancient mothers also," she wrote in her *Life of St. Brigit*, published by her company, Kenmare Publications.

Following the example of Brigid, all the Kenmare nuns were treated as equals, contrary to the prevailing practice of the time. "There are two classes of sisters in every Irish convent, and the distinction between the two is very broadly marked," she wrote. "These two classes of sisters are called choir sisters and lay sisters.

"The original idea no doubt was that those who were sufficiently educated to recite the long Latin offices of the Church, as is still the custom with sisters who belong to contemplative orders, should be spared the fatigue of household duties." On the other hand, uneducated, poor sisters were obliged to do the housework, she pointed out.

In Kenmare, the distinction was abolished. "I think it is better still to receive all on an equality," she said, "and to divide the duties and employments of the convent, according to the capacity of each; so that all, like sisters, work together for the common good and for the good of the poor."

Like St. Brigid before her, the Nun of Kenmare devoted much of her time to charitable activities, most notably to the provision of relief during the famine of 1879. From her contacts abroad, established through the popularity of her books, she raised large sums of money to help the destitute and starving of Kenmare. Seed potatoes, meal and clothing were distributed through her efforts, saving thousands of lives. "God bless her! May her shadow never grow less," one gentleman remarked.

She also railed against landlords who were more interested in ensuring the payment of rents than helping the dying. "It mattered little to them where the rents were to come from," she wrote. "The tenants may starve at home, or their children may work in America to get it, but if it is not paid, their religious feelings are deeply hurt, and they exclaim in horror at the wickedness of a race who still persist in not doing what both God and man have rendered it impossible for them to do."

Her outspokenness and candour became well known. "I believe that a great deal of the evil and injustice of life is caused by the silence of those who are either afraid or ashamed to speak out," she once said. And speak out she did, becoming one of the earliest religious to comment on the improper behaviour of priests and other senior Church figures.

"The first faint breath of suspicion that anything could be wrong in those who were devoted to the service of God came to me at this time, but I put it from me with the consoling reflection that scandals must come. Later I had to learn, to my infinite grief, that scandals of a most serious kind exist, and exist unreproved, which is the real evil," she wrote.

She was also forthright about the normally unseen and un-noticed negative character traits of priests: "I certainly have met in some priests, instances of almost childish intolerance and readiness to take offence, such as are far less common among men of the world," she noted. "One might fairly expect that the stupendous graces of their ordination and their mode of life would help to make them as truly fathers in heart as they are in name."

Nor did she hold back about nuns: "Those who enter a religious house, young, and full of hope and zeal, and with such sublime ideas of perfection, still take with them poor humanity. To believe that putting on a religious garb will at once alter the dispositions, tempers, or personal peculiarities, is a sad delusion. It is true that we may, by generous efforts, change in some respects, but nature is slow, and habit is strong."

For someone with such strong viewpoints – and a willingness to share them with others – it was inevitable that the Nun of Kenmare would encounter choppy waters in her personal and professional life. In Kenmare, she battled with landlords and the clergy, and fell out with her fellow nuns. The resulting turmoil led to her departure in 1881, following a 20-year spell in the town.

In the following years, she led a colourful life. She established an industrial school for young women at Knock, unsuccessfully attempted to establish a convent there, left the Poor Clares, founded a new order called the Sisters of St. Joseph of Peace, and eventually returned to her Anglican roots. In 1899, aged 70 years, she died and was buried in England, leaving behind memories of a nun who, not unlike St. Brigid, was energetic and charitable, independent-minded and thoughtful, and who left an indelible mark on her time.

Among the Nun of Kenmare's many publications was a book, *Cloister Songs and Hymns for Children*, published in 1881. It contains a heartfelt poem to St. Brigid, excerpts from which are featured below. She published the book under her religious name, Sister Mary Francis Clare.

LIFE OF ST. BRIGIT

For us may holy Brigit pray,
And keep us safe from harm,
Until we see God's Spirit blest,
Where fears no more alarm.

O holy Saint! who Currah's plains
Hast in thy lifetime trod;
There's none but Mary ever blessed
Has come so near to God.

In Brigit, then, oh let us trust,
She will protect us all;
For not in vain shall Erin's hosts
On holy Brigit call.

Two virgins are in heaven above,
Their client I would be;
Mary and Brigit I invoke,
Protection give to me.

In 1889, *The Irish Monthly* published a charming account of a lady's visit to St. Brigid's birthplace at Faughart. The following is an abridged version of the article, which was written under the pseudonym "M. McG."

ST. BRIGID'S BIRTHPLACE

You must let me choose the day. It shall be a day late in Spring, with a fresh breeze blowing, for we want our view to be clear and open, and withal varying, not shrouded in soft mistiness, nor steeped in too universal sunshine.

Proceeding from Dundalk on such a day, along the old highway leading from that town to Newry, we come, after two or three miles, to a narrow road turning off to our left, winding this side and that, clambering up hill and diving down again, yet in reality always ascending, till it leads us to Faughard Churchyard.

Within the enclosure of this cemetery, standing among the graves, are the ruins of a very ancient church. Examining the ruins, we find in themselves proof of their antiquity. It is said they are the remains of a church erected by St. Monenna, probably in honour of St. Brigid. I think it likely that there was also a convent of St. Brigid's order in this place.

There were then, we may be sure, numbers of pilgrims coming, as they do still, to seek the intercession of the wonder-working Saint, and in this secluded situation there would be much need of such charitable hospitality as St. Brigid herself had loved to dispense. We can fancy the nuns in their graceful robes of white ministering to the wants of pilgrims from all parts of the land.

On the opposite side of the road, some distance farther on, rises a high dun, called by the people "Faughard Moat." Tradition says that the spot covered by the ruins of the church is the site of the house where Saint Brigid was born, and tradition is supported by one of the old lives of the Saint. More modern biographers consider the dun the more likely situation.

This fort is a very high one, constructed of earth and stones, and surrounded at the base by the remains of a deep trench. The interior has not been explored of late days, but is said to contain extensive chambers. Whether it is the actual site of St. Brigid's birthplace is another insolvable question, and when we have climbed to the summit and looked at the view before us is a question we shall speedily forget.

Above us the dome of the sky seems deeper, bluer, more gloriously free and distant than ever, the fleecy clouds more dazzlingly white against that fathomless azure. Out before us stretch the shining waters of Dundalk Bay, and, bounding our view to the north, the Cooley mountains raise their summits in emulation of distant Slieve Gullion, and gaining a victory after many efforts, sink contentedly into the sea.

You may watch those fair hills the day long, and never see twice just the same tinge of colouring, or the same disposition of light and shadow. Now splendid depths of purple and blue, where the cloud shadows loiter, then delicate grey-blues, and faint yellows and greens, and pale mauves, when the clouds have passed, and the sunshine again rests on them, brightening even the sombre masses of Tippings Wood.

These beautiful heights are separated from the lesser heights of Faughard by a valley. The shadows are at work here too, casting a hazy veil of mystery on the fresh green of the fields. Looking to the other side, beyond the intervening fields, and the fir-grown ridge that marks the railway line, you see Dun Dealgan, crowned now with a thick belt of trees, guarding the busy town that lies below, between it and the sea.

But if we wish to visit those spots which tradition connects with the name of St. Brigid, we must descend from our lofty standpoint. We shall cross the road and come to a well, surmounted by a conical stone covering, now much dilapidated. A tree drops over it, and the green mounds swell high around it on three sides. To this well many come to seek, through St. Brigid's intercession, relief from headache, and from that most universal of ills, toothache.

But it is not here they make the "Station." To reach this spot, we must go farther along the road. We descend some stone steps into a thinly planted piece of ground, with a pretty stream gurgling through it. This is St. Brigid's Stream. We follow it some distance to where a tree has fallen across, and this is the spot where the Station begins.

Now there is something more to indicate this than the fallen tree – a bush covered with pieces of rag of many kinds and colours. It is in obedience to that instinct of gratitude, which prompts a return for favours received, that these curious relics have been left by pilgrims. And so they tied to a bush at hand a piece of the bandage that had covered some injured part, a sign that, through the efficacy of the Saint's prayers, it was needed no longer.

At this spot, as I have said, the Station is begun by the recital of some prayers. The pilgrims then retrace their steps through the thicket, cross the road, and descending at the other side into the field, proceed by a little track where the furze has given up all attempts at growing, and emerge at an open spot, where the stream reappears.

At this place more prayers are recited, and mortification is joined to prayer, for those performing the Station kneel, with bared knees, on one of the largest stones, which is sometimes half covered with water. This stone is indented, just as a plastic substance would be indented by one kneeling upon it; and they tell that St. Brigid was accustomed to kneel here and pray, as they do now, and that this is the miraculous impression of her knees.

When the usual number of prayers, which they count in primitive fashion on pebbles gathered from the bed of the stream, has been said, they proceed to the third and last spot, where they complete the Station with some more prayers. If the person who performs it is himself afflicted with bodily ailments, he bathes the injured part in the water. If it has been performed for another, some of the water is carried away for a similar purpose.

Regretfully we turn away from a spot we feel to be holy, sanctified, if not by the heroic action of one of God's saints, or His miraculous protection of her, yet by the faith which has been manifested here – the faith typified long ago by the "lamp in Kildare's holy fane," kept lighting through the darkness of persecution by the virtue of the women of Erin, the daughters of St. Brigid.

Thinking such thoughts, we walk through the last golden gleams of the setting sun into the dim greyness of twilight, turning now and again to catch a glimpse of the glowing sky behind us, as we will turn our thoughts many a time in moments of dim doubt and grey trouble to this bright day spent in St. Brigid's birthplace.

So many Irish women named Bridget worked as housemaids in 19th-century America that domestic staff came to be known as "Bridgets." They didn't have a good reputation.

A silent film was released in America in 1909 called *A Servant's Revenge*. The lead character was an Irish maidservant named Bridget. Having been dismissed from her job, she wasn't in a happy mood. Aware that her mistress was about to hold a dinner party, she vowed to take revenge.

Disguised as a grocer's assistant, she entered her mistress's home. First, she added a remedy for constipation to the various pots and pans simmering on the stove. She then disconnected the hose of the gas lamp in the dining room and replaced it with the water hose from the garden. Finally, she went upstairs and placed burnt cork in her mistress's box of face powder. Bridget then settled back to enjoy the fun.

The guests developed violently-disturbed stomachs. The butler flew about, searching for a doctor. A geyser of water exploded from the gas jets. The hostess, who had gone upstairs to powder her nose, returned with her face liberally coated with burnt cork. A triumphant Bridget disclosed her identity and gloated over her complete revenge.

Described as "an uproarious comedy," "a rare treat" and the "funniest thing you've seen," the movie, by all accounts, had audiences splitting their sides. They might have thought it hilarious, but not one of them was in the least bit shocked. This, after all, was exactly what Americans expected from an Irish "Bridget" – the most insolent, destructive, offensive, ill-mannered, cheeky and brazen creature ever to enter their houses and homes!

From the mid-19th century onwards, tens of thousands of young Irish girls, often named Bridget, departed for America to work as domestic servants in private homes. Many were in their late teens and early 20s; some were as young as 13 years old. They flooded the market, drawn by offers of pre-arranged employment, free accommodation and work requiring seemingly limited skills.

In 1855, in Buffalo, New York, one-quarter of Irish girls living in the city worked as live-in domestics. The pattern was similar elsewhere. These "Bridgets," as they were soon called, had come from one-room or two-room thatched cottages in Ireland, with dirt floors and primitive cooking facilities. They were now living in sophisticated homes, many of them modern mansions with up-to-date kitchens. Few knew how to cook; many were poor at interpersonal relations.

Lacking culinary skills and untrained in housework, they were soon being sniggered at and criticised not only in parlours and coffee shops but in the American press. Of particular interest to their detractors were their boldness, brassiness and upfront assertiveness, and their willingness to express personal opinions. Their unreliability and tendency to leave for other employers at the drop of a hat also generated annoyance.

Harper's Bazaar – the New York-based women's fashion magazine – was quick off the mark with its satirical jokes and remarks. One joke went as follows: "Mistress: 'When you leave, I shall want a week's warning.' Bridget: 'It's me habit, mum, merely to give a blast on the auto horn.'"

Another joke was of the same calibre: "Mistress: 'Bridget, I feel so ill I wish you would not go out today. Couldn't you get what you are going for just as well tomorrow?' Bridget: 'Faith an' oi can – tomorrow or anny day. I was goin' out to get mesilf a new job.'"

There were more jokes, too. "Mistress: 'Are you sure you'll stay with us, Bridget?' Bridget (on her hundredth job): 'Faith an' I will. Don't yez suppose I know an aisy mark whin I see wan?'"

Even *The Cleveland Leader* got in on the act: "Mistress: 'Bridget, I must object to your having a new beau every night.' Bridget: 'Thin buy betther food! One'll niver come again wance he's tackled what I have t' serve him!'"

Jokes apart – and there were many of them – the Irish "Bridgets" lived unquestionably tough lives. They worked hard, endured 12-hour days and seven-day weeks, lived in ice-cold attics, were often fed substandard food, and suffered loneliness and isolation far from their homes in Ireland. They also, through their financial remittances, paid the rent of thousands of farms in the West of Ireland.

On a broader note, they played a vital role in integrating Irish immigrants into mainstream America. While many of their male Irish counterparts lived in ethnic ghettos, the maids were in close, daily contact with wealthy and successful families, whose lifestyles they observed and copied. The information they assimilated, and the insights they learned, paid dividends later on.

Their achievements evoked the greatest admiration from the eminent American journalist and anti-slavery campaigner, James Redpath. "I have heard it said that Bridget, fresh from the bogs of Connemara, is more of a Yankee than the Yankees themselves in driving a sharp bargain for her services," he wrote in 1881.

"I have always regarded this charge as a compliment to the Irish girl. I have looked on it as an augury of good omen to our Republic, for it seemed to me to show that she was quick to adapt herself to the spirit of American institutions. It seemed to me a guarantee that her children would be sure to assimilate themselves to American nationality.

"But in Ireland I discovered the true reason for this promptitude, so to speak, of financial naturalisation: that it came not from her intellect, but her memory – because she knew what the American lady did not know, that the old folks at home were at the mercy of a class without pity and with despotic power.

"No American who has ever come in contact with landlord power in Ireland will blame Bridget for her dread of it, even if it is shown, as he may think, at his own expense.....I honour these Irish girls who go alone from the land they love.....Ireland should be known in the calendar of the Church not as the Island of St. Bridget but as the island of the saints called Bridget."

It would take many decades before the dreams and aspirations of the Bridgets would bear fruit in America. In the meantime, they, and the rest of their fellow countrymen and countrywomen, were forced to grimace as movies like *A Servant's Revenge* hit the nation's cinema screens.

"A crackerjack for laughs," the adverts proclaimed. It is "the funniest picture ever shown.....the best ever seen." Join our "delighted audiences, convulsed with laughter." Come tonight, matinee Sunday afternoon, and all for the price of a dime!

A St. Brigid-related initiative – The Biddy Club – came to prominence in late 19th-century America as households struggled to deal with their Irish servant problem. The idea was inspired by the publication of a book called *The Biddy Club*.

Author Elizabeth Strong Worthington had a bright idea in 1887. Her inspiration concerned Irish "Bridgets," whose cooking was atrocious, timekeeping abominable, baking hurried, ironing late, manners questionable, and scrubbing not up to much. That list of faults only scratched the surface, if the tenor of her subsequent book was anything to go by.

Her solution was interesting, to say the least. She set up a club of ladies who met once a week to discuss household problems pertaining principally to "the servant question." A disparate group of ladies was invited. There was the rock-solid Mrs. Hughes, described as "the best of wives, mothers, and housekeepers," whose husband was always "well fed, well sewed, and otherwise well off."

There was the Imitation Millionaire, who pretended to be rich but who was "pinched beyond a point that was pleasant." There was the Sprightly Lady, a font of strength and wisdom but who seldom betrayed what was going on in her brain. Then there were the Frivolous Young Woman and the Practical Person, whose attributes were obvious, and the Silent Ladies, whose words were fewer and more diffident than those of the other ladies.

That's not to forget the woman, wisely unnamed, who was most attractive, even magnetic. "Few girls could have had more lovers than she," we are told, "and from out of them all she chose a man who in character was directly opposed to her – abrupt, decisive, active, energetic, intellectual." In other words, the make-up of the group was exactly what you would expect in any local club or society, anywhere in the world!

The ladies discussed numerous concerns about their Bridgets, including the issue of over-familiarity. "To begin with, she came to the front door when she first arrived," one lady revealed about her new housemaid, whose real name was Bridget. "She often went up and down the front stairs, and she was constantly attempting to talk with me with the easy familiarity of an old friend." Her solution: "At the end of two days I told her that I saw she would not do for the place." She was fired.

They also discussed their maids' attire. "Many of our servants are foreigners," a lady remarked. "They come from countries where they received very small wages and dressed in homely, coarse, strong garments. Here they're paid much more, and before long they begin to ape ladies in their attire. They are not able to get the best, so they deal in the imitation, spending all their wages for even this." Another lady asked: "What can we do about it?" "Forbid it," the speaker replied.

Punctuality was another problem, especially when it came to serving up food on time. "I arose at six, intending to have breakfast at half-past seven," another speaker remarked. "Half-past seven came – eight – no breakfast. Maggie smiled in a respectful but superior manner.....It was nearly nine when at last we sat down to breakfast." In this case, the housemaid took the initiative. "She wished to live nearer her Catholic Church, and made that the excuse for leaving," the speaker explained.

The discussions went on and on, enough to fill more than 300 pages of a book. "Mrs. Hughes, let us have the resolutions, please," the Sprightly Lady said. There were 20 in total, among them: to "watch over" servants' morals, "require of them a greater perfection in their service," insist that they "wear simple, neat clothing," treat them "with justice and firmness," teach them how to "economise judiciously," and demand that they be "respectful, quiet, and orderly in their speech and action."

The book, with its insights and recommendations, created quite a stir. The reviews were ecstatic. "A bright, sprightly, sensible book," "decidedly readable," "daring in its ideals," "full of admirable suggestions," and "one of those dainty little home books that every wife and mother ought to read" were among the critics' reactions. *The Minneapolis Tribune* went even further, saying that what Adam Smith's famous *The*

Wealth of Nations had done for the economy, *The Biddy Club* could do for household life.

This latter newspaper, *The Minneapolis Tribune*, took the matter to extremes. "*The Biddy Club*, with its advocacy of scientific housekeeping and its hundreds of practical hints, fills a want so great that it has hardly been realized," an editorial in its 15 January 1888 edition claimed. It is "a book with a mission," it added.

"Bad cooking drives thousands of men to alcohol and ruin," the editorial continued. "Bad housekeeping, i.e. unsuccessful home-making, is by far the most prolific of all the causes of divorce suits and family break-ups. This may not always appear on the surface, but its truth will appear when the underlying facts are looked for." And nowhere are those facts more succinctly laid out than in *The Biddy Club*.

The book, although written by Elizabeth Strong Worthington, was brought out in 1888 under the *nom de plume* Griffith A. Nicholas. Its full title was quite extraordinary – *THE BIDDY CLUB: and how its members, wise and otherwise, some toughened and some tender-footed in the rugged ways of housekeeping, grappled with the troublous SERVANT QUESTION, to the great advantage of themselves, and, as they hope, of many others.* Despite the title, it was an instant success.

As explained in the book, the initial meetings of The Biddy Club eventually came to an end, with all agreeing that "a strong, competent, faithful servant" should never be overestimated. "She is the very salt of the earth," Mrs. Hughes proclaimed. "Briny Bridget," the Sprightly Lady murmured, in reference to the salt. "Yes," laughed Mrs. Hughes, "she may well be called briny, both for that reason, and also because she generally comes from over the sea."

With that, the conversation drifted into tittle-tattle. All the ladies offered their appreciation at the pleasure afforded them by the club and expressed the hope that they would meet again in the autumn. A vote of thanks was offered to the chairwoman for providing all present with such valuable insights. Soon after, the ladies dispersed and headed home, intending, no doubt, to pray for some much-needed miracles to redeem their troublesome Bridgets.

Two cultivated flowers – the St. Brigid's Anemone and St. Brigid's Christmas Rose – became hugely popular among gardeners in Victorian Britain and Ireland. The mystery behind why they bear the saint's name and who "invented" them is unravelled below.

It is not uncommon for the names behind great inventions to disappear in the fog of history. Few people today, for example, are aware that Adolphe Sax created the saxophone, Thomas and William Bowler were responsible for the hard felt hat, George Ferris built the popular playground ride, and the Jacuzzi family invented the large baths with underwater jets.

That observation is equally true when it comes to the famous St. Brigid's Anemone, which is commonly grown by gardeners today. It is also true in the case of the St. Brigid's Christmas Rose, which has largely disappeared from nurseries but remains no less famous. Where the connections with the saint originally came from and who initially bred them has been lost with the passage of time.

Our search for the origins of these renowned flowers begins in the parish of Carnmoney, County Antrim, not far from Belfast. It was here that Alice Louisa Bland was born in 1841. Her father was the Rev. Robert Wintringham Bland, an Anglican curate who lived in a wonderful house called Abbeyville, which had spectacular views of Belfast Lough. There was nothing modest about the property, which boasted seven bedrooms, three reception rooms, not to mention servants' quarters.

More relevantly, it contained impressive gardens, about six acres in size, with frontage to the sea. It was in these gardens that Alice Louisa, when she was young, observed her father working in the grounds and greenhouse, cultivating and preparing his flowers and plants for exhibition at the Royal Botanic Gardens Fruit and Flower Show in Belfast. She inherited her green fingers from her father, who won numerous prizes.

Her familiarity with St. Brigid arose in a different way. Her local parish church, the Church of the Holy Evangelists, was located on the site of an ancient well attributed to St. Brigid. The little river flowing nearby was also connected to the saint. Not surprisingly, when she got married – appropriately to a man from County Kildare, a landowner named Edward Lawrenson – the ceremony was conducted at her parish church.

Following their marriage, Alice Louisa Lawrenson, as she was now known, and her husband Edward moved into Sutton House, on the sheltered side of Howth Head, County Dublin. There, she indulged her passion for gardening. Set on almost 95 acres of land, she had at her disposal wonderful gardens, graperies, melon and cucumber beds, a conservatory, and gravel walks on the hill and to the sea. "The greater part of the land is very productive and in good heart," it was reported.

The local climate was ideal for gardening. The Hill of Howth provided protection from cold northerly winds, while the warm North Atlantic drift brought mild weather from the south. Freezing days, with sub-zero temperatures, were rare. Summer heat was tempered by the proximity of the sea. Rainfall was among the lowest in the country. Helped also by the favourable soil around Sutton House, she was perfectly placed for undertaking gardening experiments.

Mrs. Lawrenson was soon developing new flower varieties, including the St. Brigid's Anemone and St. Brigid's Christmas Rose. Both were wonderful to the eye. Her unique anemone – a flower of the buttercup family – was cheerful and bright, and was soon in high demand. "Providing colour from late spring to early summer every year and very easy to grow, no wonder they are so popular," a retailer proclaimed.

One gentleman who acquired samples of the anemone from Mrs. Lawrenson was ecstatic in his praise. "On entering my room the owner unfolded from a parcel in her hand some of the brightest and most charming Anemone blooms I ever saw even in April or May," he wrote in 1893. "Chrysanthemum flowers looked absolutely pale and dull and lifeless beside them, and life seemed brighter and more enjoyable for their sunny presence."

The Naturalists' Field Club of Dublin also waxed eloquently about the St. Brigid's Anemones after a "most enjoyable" visit they paid to Sutton House in 1886. "One could only liken the beds to gorgeously-coloured eastern carpets spread out in the sunshine – a poor compliment to pay to living blossoms dancing in the breezes of a delicious sunny morning in May," they remarked. Club members "swarmed like bees" among them, they added.

The anemone's popularity brought to the fore the name of St. Brigid, which Mrs. Lawrenson employed to identify her new flower. She not only used the name for that purpose, but she also used "St. Bridgid" – with its different spelling – as a *nom de plume* for her writings with the horticultural periodical *The Garden* and its rival *The Gardeners' Chronicle*. Soon, people were referring to her as "St. Bridgid, Hill of Howth," although many knew that her real name was Alice Louisa Lawrenson.

Mrs. Lawrenson also attached the saint's name to her famous Christmas rose. By all accounts, it too was a sight to see. "That's St. Brigid's Christmas Rose," a gentleman pointed out to visitors to his garden in 1884, when asked about a mass of unusual deep green foliage which had attracted their attention.

Dividing with his hands the curtain of greenery, the gardener revealed "a nest of flowers of spotless white, numbering some dozens." It was, the visitors recalled, "a revelation of floral beauty" which "made one stare and stop long to admire." Unfortunately, the Christmas rose, although widely regarded, was scarce and eventually all but disappeared.

Ten days before Christmas 1886, Alice Louisa's husband died from abdominal cancer after enduring a difficult battle with the disease over the previous six months. She remained at Sutton House for the next four years, but eventually moved to a smaller, yet no less salubrious, property named Salerno, in Killiney, on the other side of Dublin Bay.

There, in her "charming little garden," she continued to indulge her passion in a more modest way. Although no longer able to cultivate her St. Brigid's Anemones, she focused on raising daffodils and also developing her St. Brigid's Christmas Rose. Then, in 1900, aged 58, she passed away, her death certificate stating that she died from "acute double pneumonia."

Her friend, Frederick William Burbidge, the eminent plant collector and garden curator, paid her a final, glowing tribute. He wrote: "The rich variety, the vigour of growth, the brilliancy of colouring, and the perpetual flowering habit of 'St. Brigid's' race of Anemones will long serve to perpetuate her contribution of loving labour to our gardens."

There was, however, much more to this fine lady than that. Through her work, Burbidge noted, she had brought "greater happiness and contentment" to our lives. "Has not her fair hand enriched the earth?" he asked. Had not our flowers become better than before as a result of her genius? That, he concluded, was her greatest achievement.

What follows is the story of a 10-year-old boy who inspired the restoration of St. Brigid's Cathedral, Kildare, in the late 19th century.

The story of how 10-year-old Richard Chaplin kick-started the renovation of St. Brigid's Cathedral in Kildare has almost been lost to history. Only through a close scrutiny of news reports from the late 19th century can we discover details of how an initial £2.10s donation he made inspired the fundraising that saved the building from decay and destruction.

At the time, the church seemed doomed. Wave after wave of invaders had desecrated the original edifice. In 836, the Danes had ravaged and set fire to the structure, one-half of which was destroyed. They repeated their assaults, time after time, in the years ahead. Further carnage in the 17th century had left the church in ruins. Efforts to rebuild it proved fruitless. By the late 19th century, much of the building was roofless, and worship was confined to one small area.

One Sunday evening, Dr. Chaplin – Richard's father – on returning from the church said to his wife: "I think when it rains as it did tonight I shall be obliged to hold up an umbrella, as the rain was coming through the roof and falling on my head." His son, who was listening, interjected: "We will build the Cathedral up again. I have got a bullock and a calf and five or six sheep. I will sell them and give the money towards rebuilding the Cathedral."

He then asked his father: "What will you give towards it?" "£25," Dr. Chaplin replied. His mother promised the same sum. Still not happy, he turned to an old lady sitting in the drawing room. "Mrs. Tottenham," he asked, "what will you give?" "£25," she responded. On that fateful evening, the money raised by Richard Chaplin set in motion a campaign that not only saved the Church of Ireland building from ruin but turned it into the wonderful, historic Cathedral of St. Brigid which stands in Kildare today.

As a result of Richard's initiative, funds came rolling in. The Duke of Leinster contributed in excess of £2,000. Other sums were donated by local landowner Mr. Cooke-Trench, the Archbishop of Dublin, Dean of Kildare, Earl of Clonmel,

Dowager Marchioness of Bath, down to a five shillings donation made by a Mr. Christopher Bagot. The list of contributors, later published in the press, was impressive.

In 1875, a ceremony for the laying of the first stone of the new structure was held. Sunday School children assembled around the doorway of the nave, where they were joined by members of the congregation and some townsfolk. Scripture was read "in a solemn and impressive manner," it was reported. Hymns were sung and prayers offered up for God's blessing. And then, quite rightly, the first stone of the new cathedral was laid by Master Richard Chaplin.

On Tuesday, 22 September 1896, the almost brand-new Cathedral of St. Brigid was formally reopened. Fifteen hundred people crammed into the church for the historic occasion. A special train conveyed people from Dublin; a similarly large number of people arrived from the south. Although the weather was poor, spirits were high, and those in attendance were moved and inspired by the occasion.

The Archbishop of Canterbury was there. So, also, were the Archbishop of Armagh and Archbishop of Dublin, and a vast array of bishops from places including Ossory, Cork, Limerick, Meath, Glasgow, Likoma in East Africa, and Ballarat in Australia. The choir was drawn from St. Patrick's and Christ Church cathedrals in Dublin. The music was under the conductorship of Charles Marchant, organist and choir master of St. Patrick's.

The service was full choral and opened with the processional hymn *The Church's one Foundation*. As the hymn was sung, the clergy formed two lines, through which the procession passed. The strains of Beethoven's *Hallelujah*, the *Te Deum* and *Benedictus* echoed through the structure. The Epistle was read by the Archbishop of Armagh, and the Gospel was read by the Archbishop of Canterbury.

"The re-opening of St. Brigid's Cathedral, Kildare, on Tuesday last, may be termed a truly historic event in the annals of the Irish Church," *The Leinster Express* reported on Saturday, 26 September. "It is doubtful if ever there has been as imposing and distinguished a gathering of Divines and Churchmen in the Kingdom as assembled in the ancient shrine of Kildare."

The Archbishop of Canterbury, who was greeted by enthusiastic applause, was the main attraction. In his address, he praised all those, including Almighty God, who ensured that the cathedral had "been raised, almost anew, from a condition of ruin and reproach." He particularly singled out the self-sacrifice which had ensured that the project reached fruition, which must have impressed Richard Chaplin, who was seated below him.

By that stage, Richard was in his 30s, had graduated from university with a Master's degree, and had become a curate in the Church of Ireland. In that capacity, he served not only the people of Naas and Fontstown but, for a three-year period, the parishioners of St. Brigid's Cathedral, Kildare. He eventually died on 3 June 1914, bringing great sadness to the people of the town who, on the evening of his death, had been celebrating the results of recent rural elections.

When the news filtered through, up to 1,000 people had already assembled at the Market Square, where a platform had been erected, bands were performing, and a bonfire had been lit. Immediately, the celebrations came to a halt and, as *The Kildare Observer* noted, "the people all dispersed quietly, and by 10.30 pm Kildare had resumed its ordinary tranquillity and silence."

Richard's will made for interesting reading. He left the bulk of his estate to his wife, with the remainder divided among charitable institutions including Dr. Barnardo's Homes and Mrs. Smyly's Homes for Destitute Children. Unsurprisingly, he didn't forget the cathedral at Kildare, to which he left a substantial sum, replicating the generosity he had shown with the £2.10s donation he had made as a young boy almost four decades before.

Around the same time as the cathedral's restoration, Irish Catholics were intensifying their devotion to the Rosary. Most were probably unaware that their beads dated back to St. Brigid, as was pointed out earlier in this book.

In 1883, Pope Leo XIII dedicated the month of October to the Rosary. Year after year, with unflagging zeal, he exhorted the faithful to engage with fervour in this practice. From then on, hundreds of thousands of Irish families either knelt in prayer in their homes or walked through dark, gloomy autumnal evenings to their local churches where they spent half an hour, or so, in devotion and prayer.

As they knelt in those churches, they were continuing a tradition dating back to St. Brigid, who had not only commended the Rosary but had chosen the prayers and represented them on a string of beads. Thus the foundations were laid for the October devotions, which were wonderfully documented in 1894 by author Ellen Beck. She wrote about them for *The Rosary* magazine under the pseudonym "Magdalen Rock."

"THE ROSARY" IN AN IRISH COUNTRY PARISH

It is an October evening in an Irish country parish. There is a "long, gold, billowy sweep of sky" in the West where the sun has gone down, and the fields are brown and bare. In the snug haggards that surround the farm-houses their produce has been gathered, and now there is nothing to be done but to dig out the potatoes before "the coming November rains," as L. C. Irving sings.

In the dim light one can see the women and girls leaving the scenes of their labours, and hurrying homeward "to make ready," as they phrase it, for "the Rosary." Leaves of russet and red and gold are drifting from the trees with each chill blast, the wind pipes loudly amid the vocal reeds, and, as the bell of the little church proclaims that it is half-past six o'clock, groups of people begin to appear from deep boreens and meadow ways.

There is a moon almost at the full in the East, and the number of people is increased by that circumstance, for the old try to make their ten visits while there is moonlight enough to enable them to pass with some degree of security along paths made treacherous and slippery by heavy rains and fallen leaves; and now they come to the broad road that leads to the little church, that looks grey and sombre, though its long, narrow windows are all lit up.

There is an almost imperceptible pause as each group passes the low, comfortable, thatched cottage, with its little garden in front, where a few late roses and dahlias and hollyhocks still bloom, for there the curate resides, and you can hear, "We're in time after all, thank Goodness," as they notice that the lamp is burning brightly in the priest's sitting-room. They have learned from observation in this, as in many previous Octobers, that "his Reverence" turns down his lamp till it only sheds a faint glimmer ere he leaves his domicile, and there is a slight slacking of the pace that has been kept up for the remainder of the way.

"The bell rang just as we were putting the last sod on the potato pit," a young fellow remarks, wiping his brow. "Well, this is my tenth visit anyhow." "You'll need to make two or three extra," someone rejoins, "since you were late more than once, Ned." "That's sure, but I set out with a good intention, and that's everything," Ned makes answer, and so they move on past the churchyard, where cypress and yew and weeping willow cast fanciful shadows on the grave-mounds, and where the last shivering leaves on the aspens quiver.

The headstones and crosses have a ghostly look, and the little river that runs close by seems to be chanting a plaintive requiem for the dead that lie so near. Many prayers and petitions will be offered up for the fathers and mothers and husbands and wives and friends that sleep here in these last days of October.

There is something touching, yet not dismal, in those old graveyards in Ireland, with their lines of ancient elms and slender aspens, where the rooks gather at eve. There are very few expensive monuments or columns of marble raised above the dead, but plain grey stones, moss-grown and ivied, bear not one or two names, but those, maybe, of husband and wife and their children and children's children.

There are rose-bushes without number planted at nameless graves, where white lilies, too, and clove pinks bloom in the summer days, and graves where the grass grows rank and tall, and where a mourner seldom kneels. Are they waiting, those forgotten ones, I wonder, for All Souls' Day, when they too will be remembered by that mighty Mother who forgets not her children's needs?

Up the church-steps the people throng, and passing to the little chapel – a church among the Northern Irish generally means the building where Episcopalians pray – and we can see the congregation plainly. The men have come in their everyday fustians, and the women and girls wear no head-gear in the shape of hats and bonnets. They are wrapped in shawls, and not a few of the elder women wear the heavy blue cloaks that were so fashionable in the days of our grandmothers.

They are not an elegantly attired congregation, sure enough, but there can be no question as to their devotion. You can judge that by the murmur of voices, rising and falling as they make the responses when the priest recites Rosary or Litany, and when Benediction is given one recalls Aubrey De Vere's beautiful lines:

"The low wave yearns along the coast,
With sob suppressed like that which thrills,
When o'er the altar mounts the Host,
Some chapel 'mid the Irish hills."

114

But now the Angelus is said, and the people slowly disperse. The moon has mounted higher, and the sky is of a deeper blue, with clouds scattered over it that look like "carded wool." Neighbours wait on each other, and the walk home is by no means unpleasant for those hardy country folk who know pass and fell.

There are a hundred and one beautiful things to observe; from the moon "like a spirit glorified," to the half naked trees outlined against the sky, and the gleaming drops that cling to the thorns; and innocent jest and merry laugh ring out as the people pass homeward from "the Rosary."

As the 19th century came to a close, new issues dominated Irish life, among them the struggles for political freedom and sexual equality. In the vanguard of both movements was Maud Gonne MacBride, who was a devotee of St. Brigid.

In 1898, Maud Gonne paid a visit to St. Brigid's well at the end of an extended stay in Ballina, County Mayo. Although she never identified its exact location, the well was most likely at Mullafarry, a short distance from the town, where a popular holy well attributed to the saint was located.

Having toured the local famine-stricken areas and promoted the nationalist cause in Mayo, she had a few hours to spare as she awaited her departure by train from Ballina. Using the free time to visit the holy well seemed like a good idea, as she was a lifelong admirer of the saint.

Maud was led to the well by "the girls of the town," she later explained. She was keen to test its magical powers. She had been told that if anyone made a wish over its water and a fish appeared on the surface, the wish would be granted.

The legend of mysterious fish living in holy wells was widely accepted at the time. "Blessed fish," such as a salmon, trout or eel, were believed to live in their depths, occasionally appearing to those seeking an omen for the future or in search of a cure. Such appearances were rare, although regarded as greatly significant when they occurred.

Maud "wished the wish of all our hearts – a Free Republic," she later wrote in the opening paragraph of her autobiography, underlining the importance of what occurred. Suddenly, a fish appeared. "It had darted across the clear water," she said. "I had seen the fish which they said none of our generation had seen."

"Tired but glowing," Maud returned to Ballina, where there was a huge send-off at the train station, with cheering crowds and a band bidding her farewell. The Town Council made a formal address and presented her with a beautiful pedal spinning wheel made especially "for her services to the poor of Ireland." The wheel became a treasured possession, not only commemorating her visit to Mayo but as a reminder of her experience at the well.

At the time of Maud Gonne's Mayo visit, she was one of the best-known political activists in Ireland and fêted as a national celebrity. Born in England in 1866, her mother had died when she was a child and her father, an army officer, was posted to Ireland. After his death, while in her early 20s, she was drawn to the revolutionary nationalism in vogue at the time.

By then, she was said to be the most beautiful woman in Ireland. Six feet tall, with red-gold hair and hazel eyes, she had perfect features, the carriage of a goddess, and was full of charm. Among those smitten by her beauty was poet W. B. Yeats, who pursued her with intense desire. "I had never thought to see in a living woman so great beauty," Yeats remarked. "It belonged to famous pictures, to poetry, to some legendary past."

Maud Gonne's visit to Mayo in 1898 highlights two strands of the political activism which made her famous in the late 19th century. The first was her work on behalf of the poverty-stricken famine victims of Mayo, including those residing in the mountainous, boggy barony of Erris. There she witnessed "the pinched, wan faces of the men and women" and "the skeletal forms of the little children." Her lobbying for emergency food supplies, higher wages, and the free distribution of seed potatoes helped stop the famine and saved many lives.

The second strand was her nationalist agenda, including her involvement with preparations for the centenary celebration of the 1798 Rebellion. Her arrival in Ballina, where she was part of those preparations, created a lively stir in the town. Not only was she greeted from the train by a brass band, but she had become so famous that "an immense crowd waited eagerly around the railway station greatly excited at seeing Miss Gonne." Their cheering "rent the air with lavish enthusiasm," it was reported.

Maud Gonne's role in founding the Irish nationalist women's organisation Inghinidhe na hÉireann – "Daughters of Ireland" – in 1900, propelled her to even greater fame. The organisation, with Maud as President, was established under the patronage and guidance of St. Brigid. Its aims ranged from demanding full national independence and women's suffrage to more practical matters such as the provision of free meals in schools and supporting home industries.

With no money to its name, and its treasury empty, Maud argued that St. Brigid would provide. If not, she said at one meeting, another organisation she was part of, the People's Protection Committee, would step in. There was great laughter among those in attendance as that committee's membership amounted to five, and their coffers were empty, too. Instead, Inghinidhe na hÉireann turned to raising money by subscription, with remarkable success.

In the years ahead, St. Brigid dominated the organisation's activities in a multiplicity of ways. At their first ceilidh, Maud delivered a speech on "The Goddess Brigid," while another executive member later addressed the life of the saint. Members also painted and drew pictures of St. Brigid, along with legendary Celtic figures such as Maeve and Emer, and religious icons including the Virgin Mary.

Maud later took seriously the study of art which, like all Victorian upper-class girls, she had been introduced to as a child. A notable illumination she painted of St. Brigid was bought by the New York lawyer John Quinn, who was a well-known collector of modern art and who once owned the largest single collection of modern European paintings in the world. Her painting stayed in his collection up to his death.

By the time of Maud Gonne's death in 1953, her life had taken many twists and turns. She had married Major John MacBride, given birth to future Nobel Prize-winner Seán MacBride, gone through a marriage break-up, and broken W.B. Yeats' heart by her indifference to his many advances.

The poet – himself a Nobel Prize-winner – never forgot her and immortalised her in verse. Indeed, it is said that she is recalled today more for her role in his poetry than for her political and feminist activities. She, however, had a different view of how she wished to be remembered. Cathleen ni Houlihan, that mythical symbol of Irish nationalism, rested her feet on many stones, she once remarked. Looking back, Maud said she felt "blessed to have been for a moment one of those little stones."

MODERN TIMES

St. Brigid almost became the No. 1 patron saint of Ireland. She was arguably more popular than St. Patrick, a more successful miracle worker, and unlike him, she was Irish. Brigid lost out in a power struggle between Armagh and Dublin. St. Patrick was the first Bishop of Armagh; Brigid was linked to Dublin. Armagh won the battle. As a result, there would be no St. Patrick's Day parades for Brigid.

On the popularity front, Brigid was well ahead of her rival as Ireland entered the 20th century. She appealed to all classes and creeds, to rich and poor, revolutionaries and the establishment, to the liberated and the chaste.

She was popular with people who wished to bring Ireland back to the dark ages and others who saw her as an icon of progress and modernity. Above all, her name was loved by parents.

The popularity of the name Brigid peaked during the early decades of the 20th century. If you were a girl, and not called Mary, the odds were your name was Brigid.

You would be hard-pressed to find a family in early 20th-century Ireland without a child named Brigid. The name was an automatic choice for girls in areas where the saint had strong connections. Elsewhere, she vied with Mary in the popularity stakes. In any family with more than one girl, you were almost certain to get a reaction if you shouted "Brigid!"

By 1901, according to that year's census, Brigid had established itself as the second most popular name in the country, next to Mary. Ten years later, in the 1911 census, it remained in second position, again next to Mary. Unfortunately, it is difficult to track its rise before then, as census results for equivalent decades in the 1800s were lost in the burning of the Four Courts during the Civil War.

An examination of non-census data reveals just what we suspected – that Brigid was already becoming an enormously popular girls' name towards the end of the 1800s. Take one example – the results of the July 1890 examinations at the Training College of Our Lady of Mercy, Baggot Street, Dublin, which was a well-known training institute for women teachers at the time.

Among those who graduated were Brigid Cannon, Brigid Moloney, Brigid Barrett, Brigid Canavan, Brigid Downing, Brigid Kerrigan, Brigid Kavanagh, Brigid O'Connell, Brigid O'Reilly and, just to be different, Bride Walshe. While an even greater number of graduates were called Mary, and substantial numbers were called Margaret, Kate and Anne, consternation would have erupted if you shouted "Brigid!" among the class of 1890.

People not only latched on to the name, but they also used multiple derivations of it when naming – or nicknaming – their offspring. Bridie, Breege, Bríd, Bride, Biddy, Breda, Bid, or even Bee and Beesy, became fashionable. There also was Bidelia, usually shortened to Delia. Add in surnames such as MacBride, Bride and Kilbride and it seemed that the saint's name was cropping up all over the country.

Brigid was the perfect choice of name for any parent at the time. Like any great role model, the saint had all the right attributes and credentials. "We see her first as a bright, assiduous child, sharing all she has with the poor; then as an earnest girl, striving to fulfil her filial duties under difficult and complex conditions; finally, as the self sacrificing, devout woman," *The Nationalist and Leinster Times* pointed out.

She also appealed to educated parents and to parents from successful backgrounds. Her profile, once again, fitted the bill. Not only was she intelligent and good at organisation and management, but she had impressed her personality upon her time and country. That her father was said to have been of good birth helped. As a consequence, she inspired confidence in the "best and brightest" and the finest minds of the time.

The only surprise is why the name took so long to take off. It has been speculated that in earlier centuries people were reluctant to call a girl "Brigid" in the same way that they would never call a boy "Jesus", such was the reverence attached to the saint. Although the use of Jesus became popular among Spanish speakers, the tradition never spread to the English-speaking world. The use of Brigid, however, did.

The surge in Irish nationalism in the second half of the 19th century may explain at least part of the change in outlook. People learned to speak their native language, were proud of the country's cultural heritage, and took a keen interest in their saints. From then on, it became a badge of honour to have a child called Brigid.

Newspapers such as *The Nation* advocated the name's use. Along with Grace, Honor, Eva, Norah, Aileen and Cathleen, it was perfect for anyone "who wants native names for his little girls," the weekly newspaper proposed. It also suggested Moyna

– meaning "noble," "aristocratic" or "beloved" – which was another name with Irish roots.

Unlike other Irish names, the use of Brigid spread far and wide. Irish missionaries carried her name with them. From Cologne to Seville, churches were built in her honour. Most churches in Germany and many parts of France commemorated her in the Divine Office. Her feast day was celebrated on the Continent, many miles from home.

As a result, "Brigid became one of the very few Celtic names of European popularity," *The Irish Monthly* explained. "Everywhere we meet the name under various adaptations of the gentle saint who was universally known as the Glory of the Irish." Among those adaptations were Brigida in Italy, Brit in Norway, Berget in Sweden, Brygid in Poland, Priita in Finland, Brigitta in Germany, and a somewhat different-sounding Ffraid in Wales.

By the mid-20th century – especially in the 1960s – Brigid, as a name, fell out of fashion. Other saints' names also declined in popularity. The lessening influence of the Church had an impact. People also became less hidebound by values from the past.

It wasn't that Irish names disappeared altogether – far from it. Instead, the reliable choices of earlier times were at first replaced by the likes of Eithne, Sinéad, Patricia, Sheila and Fionnuala, and later by Ciara, Niamh, Orla, Aoife and Aisling.

Although no longer in the Top 100 names, Brigid never lost ground completely. Nor can we assume that it will do so in the future. Like other names, it may experience a revival. "Long may Brigid be the type of the daughters of Erin," the *Women's Suffrage Journal*, published out of Manchester, once hoped. Who knows, but that hope could well be realised in the future.

The use of pet names or derivative names for women and girls including those named Brigid became so prevalent in early 20th-century Ireland that it drove some people to distraction. The following contains a poem written in 1915 addressing the issue.

By the early 20th century there were so many parents calling their baby girls Mary, Brigid, Margaret, Ellen and Catherine among a few other select names that a method had to be devised to distinguish them from one another.

Otherwise, parishes, towns and cities couldn't function, as confusion would reign with the large number of girls responding to the same names. Nor could individual families function, given that multiple generations were often named after each other.

The result was that pet names entered common usage. Sometimes, women and girls, as they grew older, decided to amend their names of their own volition. As a result, "the same girl is often in the space of a half dozen years known by at least half a dozen fancy equivalents of the name she received at the Baptismal font," one agitated gentleman pointed out.

Under his chosen pseudonym, "Diarmuid," the gentleman in question wrote a poem, *Fancy Names*, for the Skibbereen *Cork County Eagle*, outlining his views. It was published in December 1915.

> Oh, the times are fast changing, old styles are no more,
>> We daily see fashions we ne'er saw before,
>> The name that we got when a wee little mite,
>> Is no longer considered correct or polite;
> E'en our boys, God forgive them, have learned the same

Of changing their sensible old-fashioned name,
But the ladies – dear creatures – to fashion so prone,
So oft change their names that they scarce know their own.

No longer we hear of plain Margaret or Peg,
Instead we have Marjory, Maggie and Meg,
We have Greta and Rita and Grettie and Gret,
And Madgie and Peggy and more I forget –
While of Ellen, alas! we seldom hear tell,
We have Eily and Eileen and Nellie and Nell,
And Eleanor, Helena, and Lena we hear,
And Elsie and Ellie in print oft appear.

And Mary, a name that we all should revere,
Is often ignored and cast in the sere;
By our changeable colleens 'tis bartered away,
For Molly and Polly and Masie and May.
Elizabeth's variants a small page would fill –
We have Lilian and Lizzie and Lily and Lil;
Liza, Eliza and Betsie and Bet,
Bessie and Bess and others I've met.

And Bridget, it seems, is a name that has died,
We have Bridgie and Biddy and Bridie and Bride,
And Hannah, plain Hannah, in turn has grown
To Anna, Johannah and Joany and Joan,
And cruel indeed is the hapless fate
Of that Monosyllabic Irish name Kate;
While Kathleen and Kattie and Catherine and Kit
And Katie and Cassy confuse us a bit.

Now seldom or never we hear the name Anne,

'Tis Annie, or Nancy, Nance, Nannie, or Nan,

And Janie and Jennie get preference to Jane,

But, och! all this nonsense would fill one with pain,

And the same little girl so oft twists her name,

That a friend who mistakes her is not much to blame.

Oh, girls! be careful, give fashion good bye,

You'll soon learn reason, if you only will try.

An edict to "marry or get out" was issued to its bachelor tenants by Dunshaughlin Rural District Council in 1912. The order was prompted by Bridget Brannigan, a young domestic servant from the district who had been forced to emigrate. Her name became famous far and wide.

When she was growing up, Bridget Brannigan was just another of the numerous "Bridgets" living in County Meath. Like many of her namesakes, she couldn't find a man who would marry her in her native county and was forced to move to Britain. Living in Derbyshire, she was angry with the bachelor men she left behind, who were mollycoddled and fussed over, and had no desire to marry as a result.

Bridget wrote a letter to Dunshaughlin Rural District Council in March 1912, complaining about the state of affairs regarding their bachelor tenants. "Though many were no great thing to look at, I had some hopes that one of the best of them might ask me to take care of his house for him, cook his meals, wash his shirt, and promote his comfort and happiness as only a good Irish wife can, but I was mistaken," she wrote.

Not only were these bachelors – who were mostly labourers – happily living in fine houses provided by the council, but they were refusing to marry and letting their properties go to rack and ruin. And what were the council doing? Absolutely nothing! "From the way you are going on, the squeal of a child will never be heard in the deserted houses of Dunshaughlin district," Bridget charged. It was about time, she said, that steps were taken to resolve the matter.

The council was spurred into action. A list of bachelor tenants was produced. "Look at that list of names, 69 unmarried tenants and £500 paid to Mr. Maguire to repair the houses," a leading councillor stated. He proposed that the tenants be called upon to marry within a certain date or give the reasons why they did not. Little realising the furore they were about to cause, the council ordered that the 69 tenants be informed that they must marry within three months or give up possession of their homes.

The media – especially the British press – took to the story with gleeful delight. Their headlines were eye-catching – "Order to Marry," "Marry or Go," "The Marriage Edict," "The Bachelor Hunt," "Women Scarce," "Brides for Lonely Bachelors," the list seemed endless. One "illustrated newspaper" tracked Bridget down and splashed her photograph across their pages. Many featured interviews with the bachelors.

"The English illustrated press, with its unerring finger, as usual, on the impulse of the moment, has made Dunshaughlin one of the wonders of the world," the *Evening Herald*, which was clearly cringing with discomfort, remarked in an editorial.

"Think of it – a community where marriage is compulsory; where husbands are going a-begging!"

The editorial was even more disturbed by the photographs of the tenants published for the "delectation" of English readers. "They were photographed washing, cooking their dinner, so that their loneliness might better appeal to the tender hearts of English maidens. And it must be said that the English maidens have risen very handsomely to the occasion," the editorial remarked.

The *Evening Herald* certainly had a point, as letters flooded in from English women offering their hands in marriage. The letters were sent to the chairman and clerk of the council, and to the local post office. Four Bristol girls, "thoroughly domesticated in every way, of good appearance, aged from 19 to 27 years," offered themselves as willing brides. A 29-year-old from Bayswater, "a good cook, an all-round housekeeper, short, and very sweet-tempered," also applied.

From Sussex, a young girl wrote that she was working as a kitchen maid, earned good wages, and would make a good wife. She hoped for a speedy reply. Also hoping for a speedy reply was a 28-year-old lady from Bromley, of "prepossessing appearance, dark, quite domesticated, musical, tall and slight." She was most anxious that the person responding would state his income and reveal whether he was dark or fair.

Most people agreed that the prettiest applicants were two young sisters, Iris and Doris, from Portsmouth, who were aged 22 and 24 respectively. They sent their photographs with their letters. They had a little income of their own and wished to correspond with bachelors "not exceeding 30 years of age."

They were seeking "two nice young men who must be in a decent position," they said.

Bridget, too, was deluged with offers of marriage. They came from all parts of Britain and from various Irish addresses. One came from as far away as the Gold Coast in Africa. In that letter, which was addressed to "Miss Brannigan, care of the Dunshaughlin District Council," the proposer said he was an electrician in charge of a gold mine and regarded himself as being "rather good-looking."

Other correspondents, aware from the press that women had been applying in vain to match up with the bachelors, wondered if the ladies might be willing to marry them instead. A gentleman who was moving to Canada on 11 April asked to be put in touch with a genuine applicant before that date. "Any girl of a decent age" would do, he said, but hopefully they would be "not too much of the suffragette."

Newspapers sent reporters to Dunshaughlin to assess the scene. A bachelor tenant, aged between 50 and 60, was blunt when interviewed. "I'll marry when I like," he said, "and I'm going to take no orders from anyone as to when I will get married." Another person, a woman in her 70s, spoke on her brother's behalf, explaining that he was aged 72. "Micky doesn't want any wife at his age," she said. A labourer, on 12 shillings a week, remarked that he couldn't afford to be married.

Some relented and decided to tie the knot. By mid-May, a month before the three-month deadline expired, six of the men had married, leaving 63 still sitting on the fence. By June, the patience of the council was running thin. They asked their rent collectors to supply a list of bachelors living alone, with a view to enforcing eviction orders. A few weeks later, they softened and extended the deadline to 1 November.

November came, and still the wound of unmarried bachelor tenants festered in the chambers of Dunshaughlin Rural District Council. By then, only ten of the bachelors had married. "The time-limit expires tomorrow, and there has not as yet been an eleventh-hour rush for marriage licences on the part of those who prefer their cottages to the charms of single-blessedness," a report in *The Globe* noted on the eve of deadline day.

From then on, the matter got ugly. Rather than backing down in the face of adverse publicity, the council proceeded with its edict. Occupants who refused to marry were given notice to quit. One bachelor tenant, James Kelly, a rural labourer, had proceedings issued against him. When the case came before the magistrate, he announced that he had been married the day before. His argument cut no ice. The solicitor for the council pressed for a decree for possession of his cottage, and it was granted.

There was ugliness in other ways, too. An eviction notice was served on a cottage occupant because his wife, in her desire to supplement her husband's meagre earnings, carried on a little dressmaking. One councillor said he had noticed a couple of bottles of sweets for sale in their window; another said he had noticed some sugar-stick. That spirit of industry and energy didn't go down well, and the discoveries proved fatal.

By then, Bridget Brannigan had long lost interest in her gripe with the council and the tenant bachelors of Dunshaughlin. It was said that she had received 120 proposals as a result of her letter but, as one newspaper reported, "the right man has not yet turned up." The council hadn't forgotten her, however, and her name cropped up in proceedings from time to time over the following years.

What is almost certain is that Bridget never returned to County Meath. It would have been difficult for her to have done so, as in her widely-publicised letter she had nailed her colours to the mast. "I may never expect to see my native place again," she wrote, "for I can marry a decent, hardworking Englishman any time I like, not a lazy bowsie, too common in Ireland." The bachelors of Dunshaughlin are "hopeless cases every one," she remarked, before signing off, "I remain, yours truly, Bridget Brannigan."

St. Brigid's patronage was invoked by British and Irish suffragettes in their efforts to secure votes for women. A nationwide day of prayer was held on her feast day in 1913.

Violence erupted on British streets in the lead-up to St. Brigid's Day 1913. In January, the suffragettes went on the warpath. Parcels and letters containing tubes of phosphorous were tossed into post boxes, setting them on fire. Pepper was flung into a policeman's face. One activist, an actress, discharged lead bullets from a catapult while seated on the upper deck of a London bus, hitting the Westminster Palace Hotel.

Attempts were made to storm the House of Commons. Six windows were smashed at Lambeth Palace, the London residence of the Archbishop of Canterbury. British Prime Minister Herbert Henry Asquith was heckled, prompting a baton-charge by police. A jewel case was damaged at the Tower of London. When arrested, the suffragette was told by Beefeaters that they had experienced "no trouble at the Tower since 1885."

Golf greens were torn up by sharp implements and corrosive liquids, resulting in an editorial in *The Suffragette*, the official organ of the movement. "One indignant golfer protests against this action on the ground that golf brings into play mental faculties that make for the betterment of the race," the newspaper remarked. "We have not, we regret to say, observed any beneficial effect upon the faculties of the politicians addicted to this game."

St. Brigid's feast day, 1 February 1913, brought a change in tactics. The suffragettes' battle was moved from the streets to houses of prayer. "By arrangement with various bodies interested in the Suffrage Question, February 1st, St. Bride's Day will be held as a day of special meditation and intercession in Westminster Abbey, in St. Paul's, and in various cathedrals, chapels and churches throughout Great Britain," the movement announced in the press.

They had chosen the date well, they believed. Their patron, St. Brigid, was the ideal role model for emancipated women. Independent, successful and authoritative, she could hold her own with men great and small. She had spirit and good common sense. Both sexes were welcomed in her religious community. "Never around one name was gathered a greater treasure of legend and history," the suffragette leadership claimed.

On that day in February 1913 – a windy, unsettled Saturday – suffragettes gathered at various houses of prayer to reflect, meditate and pray for St. Brigid's intercession in their struggle to secure the vote. Militant and non-militant suffragettes, wearing their different badges, attended. They gathered in ever-changing groups from early morning to evening, entering and leaving in hushed flows. "The idea was a good one," the influential *Harper's Weekly* proclaimed.

It was mainly in Anglican churches that the suffragettes gathered, having been discouraged by the hostile response of the Catholic Church to their cause. The reigning Pope – Pius X – had made his views clear in a discussion with an Austrian feminist: "Women electors, women deputies? Oh, no! Women in Parliaments! That is all we need," adding, "The men have already caused enough confusion there!"

The Papal encyclical *Rerum Novarum* had also made clear that a woman's place was in the home. "A woman is by nature fitted for home-work, and it is that which is best adapted at once to preserve her modesty, and to promote the bringing up of children and the well-being of the family," it had declared in 1891. Comments such as these were not exactly what the suffragettes wished to hear!

In Ireland, the patronage of St. Brigid was also invoked by at least some of the organisations fighting for women's rights. Emphasis on the word *some* is necessary as the movement was split between non-militants and militants, and between unionists and nationalists. The Irish Catholic Women's Suffrage Association, for example, operated "under the patronage of St. Brigid." Other organisations either claimed the patronage of Joan of Arc or no patronage at all.

Those splits didn't stop violence erupting on the streets. Windows were smashed in at least one Dublin politician's home, while 16 panes of glass were shattered in Dublin Castle, the seat of the British government's administration in Ireland. Corrosive acid was poured into Dublin post boxes, and their contents were extensively damaged. "In all cases, the same destructive material was used, this being corrosive acid in uncorked bottles. Around the bottles Suffragette leaflets were found," reported *The Freeman's Journal*.

The advent of World War I, in 1914, changed everything. "So ends, for the present, the war of women against men," wrote Emmeline Pankhurst, the iconic British suffragette leader, in the late summer of 1914. The activist, who was well known in Ireland from a tour she had earlier undertaken, added: "The struggle for the full enfranchisement of women has not been abandoned; it has simply, for the moment, been placed in abeyance."

Even at that early stage of hostilities, Pankhurst could read the future. "The men are turning to their women and calling on them to take up the work of keeping civilisation alive," she remarked. "Through all the harvest fields, in orchards and vineyards, women are garnering food for the men who fight, as well as for the children left fatherless by war. In the cities the women are keeping open the shops, they are driving trucks and trams, and are altogether attending to a multitude of business."

When the war is over, will men "forget the part the women so nobly played?" Pankhurst asked. As it turned out, men – or at least the institutions representing them – didn't forget. The Representation of the People Act of 1918, at war's end, granted votes to women in both Britain and Ireland, subject to qualifications including that they be over 30 years of age. Later, full voting rights were ceded to women in both territories. But that is to jump ahead. There were, in the meantime, many other battles to fight, and St. Brigid would be at the centre of them, too.

The infamous Dublin lockout began in the late summer of 1913. Inspired by St. Brigid, the Irish Women Workers' Union found itself at the centre of the dispute.

On Tuesday, 26 August 1913, Dublin's tramway drivers and conductors defiantly pinned their Irish Transport and General Workers' Union badges to their lapels, and stepped down from their trams. By 11 o'clock that morning, the line along Westmoreland Street and Sackville Street was blocked by motionless, empty tramcars.

The strike action was prompted by a demand from the Dublin United Tramway Company's owner William Martin Murphy that employees forswear membership of the ITGWU or be dismissed. Instead of forswearing, they walked off the job. In retaliation for their action, Murphy locked them out. A wave of strikes and lockouts followed, resulting in the most poisonous labour dispute in Irish history.

Dublin was in turmoil. There were pickets, rallies, inflamed meetings, mass demonstrations and hunger strikes. Workers and their families were reduced to living on four or five shillings a week. Gangs of strikers hunted down "scabs." Rioting broke out, followed by police baton charges. Arson attacks took place. James Larkin, leader of the ITGWU, declared, "I am out for revolution, or nothing."

Women, too, became involved, including 600 at the biscuit makers, Jacob's. Signs were erected in the factory banning the wearing of union badges. Pickets were placed outside, and violence erupted. A 16-year-old girl was arrested for punching a strike-breaker who passed the picket line. In solidarity with Jacob's workers, Dublin dockworkers refused to handle the company's goods and were dismissed from their jobs, thereby escalating the dispute.

At the vanguard of the women strikers was the Irish Women Workers' Union. Formed in 1911, it was set up because other unions excluded women workers. Its members were soon manning picket lines, working in soup kitchens, and involved in mass demonstrations while bearing banners declaring "Women Workers Locked Out by the Sweating Employers of Dublin." They did all this using St. Brigid as their "exemplar" and "inspiration."

St. Brigid, the IWWU argued, was no different from the working women of 1913. "She was born of poor and simple people, and was herself a simple worker, tending the cattle, milking the cows morning and evening, driving them to and from the pasture," the union declared in its manifesto.

The manifesto continued: "We take her as our exemplar and our inspiration. We take the story of her life as a reinforcement of our faith that we, the workers of Ireland, may one day lead our country to the same high place in the world that she held in olden times."

By any standards, the working women that the IWWU represented had a worthy cause. At a time when the average wage was 18 shillings a week, the rates for women were considerably lower. In some Limerick factories, female workers earned three shillings and six pence to five shillings a week. Apprentices in the millinery and dressmaking sectors were paid overtime rates of one penny or two pennies per hour.

In Dublin, the average wage for women was six shillings and six pence per week, around one-third of the amount paid to men. Half-time work and contract work were an added problem. So, also, was the practice of outsourcing work to women at home. One woman from the North of Ireland, in 1913, described how she was familiar with a mother who, along with her children, "sat up until one o'clock in the morning trying to get their work done."

These low wages and bad conditions, along with a ban on union membership, were the main cause of women workers' discontent. Deeper causes were the apprenticeship system and the prevalence of slums, a Dublin-based women's activist, Miss Browning, argued. "Slums deadened the senses" and caused untold problems, she said. She could not understand why slum properties – worm-eaten, mouldering, patched and plastered tenements – were not being demolished.

The IWWU made headline news when one of its members, 16-year-old Alicia Brady, who had been locked out of Jacob's during the dispute, was struck by a strike-breaker's ricocheting bullet. She had been walking home with food for her family in December 1913 when she was shot. Having contracted tetanus from her wound, she died on New Year's Day 1914 and was buried at Glasnevin Cemetery.

Coming just two weeks before the lockout ended, the burial was a memorable and emotional occasion. Thousands attended. Among them were 500 members of the Irish Women Workers' Union, who wore crêpe on their arms and bore wreaths and a banner draped in black. James Larkin, James Connolly and Countess Markievicz were in attendance. The procession was headed by the ITGWU band. A large number of stewards carried draped staffs.

Larkin delivered a moving address, saying that Alicia had been "sacrificed on the altar of sweating, misery and degradation." She had shown great strength of character, he remarked, and if she had lived she would have been a great woman. James Connolly added that every "scab" and every employer of a "scab" in Dublin was morally responsible for her death. Following the burial, the procession re-formed and proceeded to Liberty Hall.

One hundred years later, a poignant event was held to commemorate Alicia's death. Alicia's niece, Brigid Taylor, who bore the same first name as the IWWU's patron saint, spoke at the ceremony. Like the funeral which was held exactly a century before, it was a memorable and sad occasion.

Brigid recalled that her mother had never forgotten Alicia and had "told all her family about her." Brigid also spoke of both Alicia and the man who shot her, along with all those who suffered during and after the lockout. "They were set against one another by people who should have known better and who had so much," she remarked. "May Alicia and all who suffered rest in peace," she concluded.

The discovery of Brigid's personal hand-bell in 1913 caused a sensation in the Somerset town of Glastonbury. It's a story without a happy ending.

The low-lying moors around Glastonbury, with their wetlands and reed swamps, are known as the Somerset Levels. It was in these moors, in a small farmhouse, that an old man died in 1913. His effects eventually came up for sale in an auction, which was attended by a close friend. The friend, it was said, had been very fond of the old man and wished to buy "something that belonged to him" to remember him by.

A man of limited means, the friend was outbid for everything on sale, bar one item. It was a small, very old, ordinary-looking oak box, which was going for five shillings. He bought it and brought it home. On opening the box, he discovered it contained an object wrapped in old linen. His curiosity aroused, he unwrapped the linen to see what was inside.

The object he discovered was a small, ancient hand-bell constructed from a sheet of bronze. The bronze sheet was folded over with the edges riveted together, thus forming the body of the bell. A ring was inserted in the bell to hold a clapper, which would be used to strike it and make it ring, but the clapper was missing.

The handle, which was made of brass, consisted of two loops for the insertion of fingers. Interestingly, the loops could only fit the fingers of a woman. The mouth of the bell was crudely rounded, but that didn't matter – when struck, the bell issued what was later described as "a very rich and musical tone."

The new owner recalled that Brigid had left her hand-bell behind following her visit to Glastonbury in 488. William of Malmesbury, the leading English historian of the 12th century, had confirmed that claim, stating that on her return to Ireland she had not brought with her "certain important relics, namely, her hood, beads, hand-bell and weaving tools." John of

Glastonbury, writing in the 14th century, concurred with that view.

The owner was also made aware that the bell, which would have been used by Brigid to call people to church or to ring the Angelus, had been made by a friend of hers, St. Gildas, who was a renowned maker of bells. He had presented it to her as a token of his esteem. Unfortunately, it had disappeared at some unknown time down through the centuries – until now, it seemed.

The newly-discovered bell generated much excitement and interest in Glastonbury, especially when, after scrutiny by specialists at the British and Dublin museums, among other notable experts, it was proclaimed that not only was it an ancient Celtic bell, similar to one owned by St. Patrick, but there was good reason to believe it had belonged to St. Brigid.

Not surprisingly, an enormous demand arose for the bell. In February 1924, for example, a choral celebration was held at St. Patrick's chapel, whose churchyard had once echoed to the sound of Brigid's feet. The little chapel, shimmering with coloured vestments and lights, was packed to capacity, which was not surprising given that this was its first choral celebration since the Reformation.

"The Celtic bell, which is known locally as 'St. Bride's Bell,' was rung outside the Chapel in the Churchyard where St. Bride possibly rang it herself 1400 years ago," a local newspaper, *The Central Somerset Gazette*, reported. "In the evening at 6 p.m. there was a special Choral Service, with a short address by the

Vicar on St. Bride at St. Patrick's. The choir was that of the boys of the Parish Church Choir. They sang beautifully."

Although that may be presumed to signal a happy ending, unfortunately it was not to be. To begin with, the new owner of the bell died and the bell came into the possession of one of his relatives. She, in turn, loaned the bell to Alice Buckton, a well-known poet and playwright from the time, who lived in Glastonbury.

Buckton had a passionate regard for Brigid and had once written a play called *The Coming of Bride*. She developed an even fonder regard for the saint's bell, which she used during ceremonies at the Chalice Well, her hostel and college for women dealing with art, music, drama, crafts and "lofty thought."

Throughout the time she had the bell, Alice kept "a dragon's watch" over it, her vicar later said. She became so attached to it that even as she aged and suffered ill health, she refused to hand it back. Then, in December 1944, Alice died, and the whereabouts of the bell died with her. It was never seen again.

Every effort was made to trace the bell by Buckton's executors and, in particular, by the Rev. Lionel S. Lewis, Vicar of Glastonbury, who offered a reward for its return. "A £25 reward is offered to anyone who can give information to the Rev. Lionel S. Lewis, the Vicarage, Glastonbury, leading to the recovery of St. Bride's Bell, which has been missing since the death of Miss A. M. Buckton," the local press reported in February 1949. Sadly, the appeal fell on deaf ears.

Whether Miss Buckton gave the bell to someone else, buried it for safekeeping, or indeed hid it in fear of a German invasion during World War II, is unknown to this day. All we do know is that the vast multitudes who have attended contemporary Glastonbury festivals, with their famous pop concerts, may have witnessed some of the finest rock bands in history, but they are unlikely to have heard the sweet sound of St. Brigid's hand-bell floating in the Somerset winds.

Dr. Kathleen Lynn, a devotee and admirer of St. Brigid, acted as Chief Medical Officer of the Irish Citizen Army during the 1916 Easter Rising.

Those who survived the 1916 Easter Rising always remembered the heat – not just the heat of battle, but the warmth of the unseasonably good weather. Although it was late April, it could have been the height of summer. Many felt the weather was like the middle of June; even better than some June months, they said.

Staff assigned to City Hall, on that morning of 24 April, despaired as they noted the beautiful day outside. Being stuck in stuffy offices – some of them Victorian; others medieval – intensified their regret. "We were even more sorry for ourselves later on, when we saw what a day it turned out to be," one who was there later recalled.

Around noon, mayhem broke out. A detachment of the Irish Citizen Army, including Chief Medical Officer Dr. Kathleen Lynn, attempted to force entry to the building. An armed policeman and a sentry blocked their way. The sentry fired his gun to raise the alarm and the policeman sprang to close the gate. The policeman was shot just as the clock struck twelve. He became the first casualty of the Easter Rising.

Having forced their way inside, a hail of gunfire erupted in the area around City Hall. Nurses in the adjoining hospital spoke of the deafening noise. Sniper fire was directed at the building from the nearby Dublin Castle clock tower. One of the bullets struck the rebel commander, Seán Connolly, killing him instantly. Lynn, who saw him fall, later remarked: "First aid was useless. He died almost immediately."

Although her fellow rebels were overwhelmingly Catholic, Kathleen Lynn was a devout member of the Church of Ireland. A rector's daughter, from County Mayo, she was a believer in "the communion of saints," her favourite saint being St. Brigid. Inspired by St. Brigid's "Gaelic" credentials and independent nature, she spoke of being "near" to her and being one of her admirers.

Her devotion to Brigid was shared by her predominantly Catholic friends and colleagues in the Irish Citizen Army. Even Countess Markievicz, an Anglican, who accompanied her to City Hall – they travelled together in Lynn's car – was enthralled by the saint. Later, the Countess converted to Catholicism, but not Lynn. On that day in 1916, however, both would no doubt experience "the feeling of the nearness of S. Brigid," as Lynn later put it.

They would need all St. Brigid's help they could get to cope with the events that unfolded later that day. All available troops from the Portobello, Richmond and Royal barracks were ordered to proceed to City Hall. More troops arrived by train from the

Curragh. Machine-guns were put in place and, from about four o'clock, a mass attack, which also involved hand-grenades and bayonets, was launched.

At one stage, Lynn looked out the window and saw what she thought was rain or sleet outside. She soon realised it was a hail of bullets. The thunder of the guns became deafening. The building shook, plaster fell from the ceiling, sending up clouds of white dust. Lynn sat in the shelter of a pillar, caring for a wounded man. He begged her not to leave him.

Lynn was in the hall of the building when the soldiers rushed in. She was accompanied by a small group of Irish Citizen Army women and the wounded man. The men of the garrison were still firing from the roof. She stood well back in the shadows of the hall, lost in the darkness.

An officer advanced into the dim, dusty light, and with a revolver in his hand shouted: "Anyone here? Speak or I'll shoot!" Lynn stepped forward and, as the next in command, surrendered the garrison, her only demand being that the wounded man be brought to hospital first. Her active role in the 1916 Easter Rising had come to an end.

Following her arrest, Lynn was detained at Ship Street Barracks, beside Dublin Castle. The accommodation was appalling and the beds were covered with lice. The women prisoners ran the gauntlet of coarse and brutal jeers from soldiers, although they bore the treatment well.

"The women took it splendidly," an observer noted. "They ignored the offensive taunts, and during their scant term of exercise danced Irish dances with as much appearance of carefree delight as if they were at some kindly *ceilidh* of the old days."

Kilmainham Gaol was different. After being transferred there on 1 May, she heard the leaders of the Rising being shot. It was "a harrowing experience," she later remarked. From there, she was moved to Mountjoy Gaol, and then deported to England, where she briefly worked as a doctor before returning to Dublin towards the end of 1916.

Kathleen Lynn's finest day in medicine was yet to come. In despair over the medical and social conditions facing poor families in Dublin, she co-founded St. Ultan's Hospital for Infants in the city in 1919. Following the example of Brigid, it catered primarily for the poor. It also became the only Irish hospital to be exclusively managed by women.

The hospital was named after a saint who was reputedly the maternal uncle of Brigid. As the seventh-century Abbot-Bishop of Ardbraccan in County Meath, he was known for his concern for the poor and the care of sick children. He particularly looked after children during an outbreak of yellow plague and, having designed a feeding device using cows' teats, which he then filled with milk, he is credited with the invention of the first baby's feeding bottle.

St. Ultan's Hospital for Infants became Lynn's pride and joy. She devoted herself to it until her death in 1955. Long before she died, back in 1916, a friend paid tribute to her. The friend chose her words well: "As an honourable Christian lady, a true woman in every sense of the word, and as a friend whom one might 'grapple to the heart with bars of steel,' the present generation has seen few equals of Dr. Kathleen Lynn, and no superiors."

The League of St. Brigid was set up in 1920 for Irish women who objected to "indecent and immodest" fashions, especially those being imported from abroad.

Short hemlines, straight waists, cloche hats and bob hairstyles were fashionable in the Roaring Twenties. Knee-length dresses exposing legs and arms were in vogue. Loose clothing, slim figures and cosmetics were the must-haves of women who danced, drank, smoked and even voted. Drab was out, fun was in, and glamour was all the rage.

Although Ireland couldn't match London or Paris in the fashion stakes, it did make the effort. Skirts would be tighter, hemlines not half as long, and hair clipped shorter, Irish women were told by the fashion press. "Where on earth do they manufacture this thing called 'fashion'?" one regional newspaper columnist asked. "We will shortly have our young girls going about with not enough clothes on them to save a moth from starvation."

A traveller by train from Kerry to Dublin was shocked by the new fashions. What was he confronted with in his train compartment? Seven women mostly with dresses above the knees, when seated, providing a display of knee caps. "Unless a man keeps his eyes glued on his newspaper, sometimes shocking, indecent sights meet his gaze – the cause of immediate occasion of sin," he remarked.

The Roman Catholic Bishop of Meath, Laurence Gaughran, was worried. "In the case of women," he said in 1920, "it is a scandal to dress immodestly, with short and slashed skirt, or with uncovered neck and shoulders, as, unfortunately, is the fashion in Ireland today.....no fashion can excuse a woman from sin who dresses in such an immodest way." His colleagues in the hierarchy concurred.

Into the picture stepped Mary Maher from Moyvoughley, County Westmeath. A wealthy widow, in her mid-70s, she was known for her religious and charitable work, and for her writings in Catholic publications. The Holy See had conferred on her a gold medal engraved with "Pro Deo et Ecclesia," meaning "For God and the Church." Unfortunately, she had lost the medal during Easter Week 1916, at the burning of the Gresham Hotel, where she was a guest at the time.

At her initiative, the League of St. Brigid was established in January 1920 with the express purpose that members would forego the wearing of foreign, indecent and objectionable fashions, and to hand down to future generations a high standard of womanly dignity. Interested women were to register at selected convents, with the initial signing-up period scheduled for 10 – 24 January.

Members were asked to make the following pledge: "For the glory of God and the honour of Erin, I promise to avoid in my own person all impropriety in the matter of dress and to maintain and hand down the traditional and proverbial purity and modesty of Irish womanhood." No subscription was required, and it was hoped that a meeting would be held in the autumn which delegates from each diocese would attend.

The League of St. Brigid was embraced with open arms by Dr. Gilmartin, Archbishop of Tuam. "The simple flowing dress of the Mother of God and the white flowing dress of Brigid" were the only proper models of chastity, he claimed. "I would ask you today, the ladies of Tuam, to join the League of St. Brigid and to stamp out any foreign fashions not consistent with the delicate female modesty which is the fairest ornament of woman."

The League was also welcomed by the press. *The Drogheda Independent* expressed the view of the man on the street: "It is not so long ago since we heard of a young man's comment on a woman arrayed in the latest up-to-date fashion. It was spoken in a tone of supreme disgust and it phrased itself thus: 'D... her, why doesn't she dress herself!' With which emphatic sentiment his companion expressed his full assent. And this was not a solitary case by any means."

The publicity had the desired effect. Some 10,006 women were said to have registered from 10 – 24 January, just in time for the forthcoming feast of St. Brigid. A further 12,002 enlisted in the period leading up to the feast of St. Patrick. That total of 22,008 grew by even more in the period up to the feast of St. Columcille. The achievement had been realised "entirely by 'Irishwomen' for 'Irishwomen,'" founder Mary Maher said, and was the result of "honest-hearted work."

If nothing more, the League generated a national debate over the correctness, or otherwise, of modern dress. The abuse was vicious. "The painted and powdered beauties of the Grafton St. type" were pilloried by letter writers in the press. Ladies who wore "doubtful fashions," played cards and backed horses were described as the "shoneenie" of Ireland.

Words like modesty, decency, impropriety were tossed about with gay abandon. Clean-living, church-going, confraternity-loving country girls were praised to high heaven. To the contrary, women who aped the fashions of "the demi-mondaines of the Continent" by wearing tight skirts and low-necked blouses while smoking cigarettes were torn to shreds.

Men became experts on what women should wear. "In my opinion they should be covered from, at least, the top of the chest to the ankle top – an inch more would be even better," one patronising male suggested. "In the matter of tightness of dress there is not so much room for transgressing decency..... No one can morally object to loose-fitting garments, and they are healthier, in my opinion."

Another man was of a similar persuasion. "The girl that every boy hopes to marry some day is modest and good as well as useful," he wrote. "The average sensible man can't be bothered with a dressed-up doll all his life. It's too expensive and, besides, he wants somebody who is a real partner. He has no use for an individual whose main object appears to be to act as a 'star turn' in the comedy of life!"

Fashion-conscious women, on the other hand, wished that men would mind their own business. "We are pestered with their attentions," one letter writer remarked. "The chaps are sneering at our short skirts. Are they not far healthier than the trains worn by our mothers? What harm is it to 'bob' the hair? Is it not less weight to carry? If veils were banished, too, we would not be a penny the worse.....Thank God we are emancipated."

Although the League of St. Brigid survived through the 1920s, its activities were curtailed by events taking place on the national stage. Just over two months after its foundation, the Lord Mayor of Cork, Tomás MacCurtain, was shot dead, Bloody Sunday followed soon after, and the country was plagued by executions, assassinations, and the outbreak of civil war. People had other things on their minds beyond fashion.

The League's final death knell was sounded in May 1930 with the passing of Mary Maher at her home, Moyvoughley House, County Westmeath. She was remembered for many things, including her literary work and intense religiosity. Most importantly, however, she was recalled for what a regional newspaper referred to as her role leading "St. Bridgid's Modest Dress and Deportment Crusade."

They were referring, of course, to her League of St. Brigid, that quaint, for a time moderately-successful, yet ultimately doomed, attempt "to bring Irish women back from the paths they are sadly, sinfully, straying in and make them the beautiful true daughters of Erin," as one of her enthusiastic followers once remarked.

Irish dramatist and folklorist Lady Gregory wrote a play about St. Brigid. It was premiered at Dublin's Abbey Theatre in 1924.

A star-studded cast took to the stage of the Abbey Theatre for the opening night of Lady Gregory's *The Story Brought by Brigit*. It may well have been the finest group of actors ever to appear at the theatre. Among those featuring that evening, 15 April 1924, was Barry Fitzgerald, the future Academy Award-winner, who went on to appear in films such as *How Green was my Valley* and *The Quiet Man*.

Also on stage was Sara Allgood, who later acted in many Alfred Hitchcock films and was nominated for an Academy Award for her performance in *How Green was my Valley*. The rest of the cast was equally impressive, including F. J. McCormick, whose onscreen role as a corner-boy in *Odd Man Out* was praised as being "outstanding"; and Arthur Shields, who had fought in the 1916 Rising and who eventually appeared in films such as *She Wore a Yellow Ribbon* with John Wayne.

The production that night – the story of Christ told through the eyes of St. Brigid – brought the house down. Poet W. B. Yeats thought it was Lady Gregory's finest play. His brother, the painter Jack Yeats, admired it enormously. Future President of Ireland Douglas Hyde said it was 20 times better than anything she had written before. And Thomas MacGreevey, the poet and critic, cried his eyes out.

The Story Brought by Brigit was based by Lady Gregory on folk tales she had collected in remote villages near her home in County Galway. She was a tireless folklorist, frequently travelling from her estate, Coole Park, into the nearby mountains. There she gathered myths and fables that had been carried seamlessly down through the ages. She recorded them with passionate zeal. She would later use these stories as the basis for her books and plays.

The legends she heard about Brigid were extraordinary. People spoke of her being "the foster-mother of Christ" and claimed that she had helped Mary and her child when they were brought to Ireland for safety from Herod. Having heard those stories, Lady Gregory decided to relate the life of Christ through Brigid's eyes. As a highlight, her Brigid travels to be with Christ at his crucifixion, having had a vision that he was in trouble.

Like other Lady Gregory plays and stories, her drama used a form of speech referred to as "Kiltartanese." The word was derived from the townland of Kiltartan, County Galway, where the playwright's home, Coole Park, was located. The English there was spoken by country people who thought in Irish, and was delivered in picturesque turns of phrase and with "a quaint, unreal ring," it was said.

Some people found Kiltartanese laughable, boorish, rustic, and disparagingly referred to it as stage Irish. "There is a hurry on me," Judas says when asked to stop for a minute. "The story is the breaking of my heart to me," another character remarks. Those lines, and many more, when spoken by Roman centurions, beggars, lads from the hills of Judea and scribes in the house of Caiaphas, were all delivered in the accents of Kiltartan!

Despite the jarring language, the play did well at the Abbey. "Her success is great," *The Freeman's Journal* remarked. The cast represented "all that is best in the Abbey Company," another review noted. Pretty much every critic concurred, remarking that Sara Allgood was "magnificent" while the other future stars of the screen, Barry Fitzgerald, F. J. McCormick and Arthur Shields, were highly praised, too.

Following the 1924 production, *The Story Brought by Brigit* was put into cold storage by the Abbey. By then, Lady Gregory was in her early 70s and the best of her writing days were over. Her output, which included translations of many Irish legends, fantasies based on folklore, peasant comedies, and nearly 40 plays which she had written or translated, had been nothing short of prodigious, but her talents were fading and her days were numbered.

In May 1932, aged 80, Lady Gregory passed away at her home in County Galway. The tributes were effusive. Lennox Robinson, the dramatist and theatre producer, called her "the most distinguished Irishwoman that ever lived." The author George Russell (AE) remarked that she had "a great splash of genius" and was "a very noble lady." Although most other commentators agreed, there was no rush to re-launch her plays on the Abbey stage.

That changed in 1939, when on the eve of World War II *The Story Brought by Brigit* appeared once more at the Abbey, with another stellar cast. Once again, replicating 1924, a surprising number of actors in the new production went on to great success. Wilfrid Brambell, who played Judas, later starred as one of the joint leads in *Steptoe and Son* on TV and also played Paul McCartney's grandfather in The Beatles' *A Hard Day's Night*.

Joe Linnane, who played the fiery zealot Silas, delivered a "vigorous performance" in the 1939 Holy Week production. Linnane was soon on his way to Radio Éireann, where he became a national celebrity as presenter of the station's *Question Time* during the 1940s and '50s. Brid Ni Loingsigh, the Kerry actress, who played Brigit, became a great Abbey star in roles such as Pegeen Mike in *The Playboy of the Western World* and as Ansty in *The Tailor and Ansty*.

Then, of course, there was Cyril Cusack, who went on to become the grand old man of Irish theatre while appearing in numerous films, including *The Spy Who Came in from the Cold*, *The Taming of the Shrew* and *The Day of the Jackal*. He received an Oscar nomination for his role in *The Blue Veil*, which he starred in with Jane Wyman.

One way or another, there certainly was something magical about that play by Lady Gregory. It may have dated quickly but, no doubt about it, it left a lot of theatrical and cinematic stardust in its wake!

St. Brigid inspired the first "Buy Irish" campaign. It was initiated in early 1931, at a time when the Irish economy was sinking to its knees.

In March 1931, a ladies' tea party was held at the fashionable Aberdeen Hall in Dublin's Gresham Hotel. The event was attended by the wives of Ireland's great and good. Up to 100 ladies – the spouses of senior political, legal and business figures – had been invited with the express intention of establishing a ladies' campaign for the purchasing of Irish-manufactured goods.

The hostess for the occasion was the diminutive, solidly-built Mrs. W. T. Cosgrave, wife of the President of the Executive Council of the Irish Free State and mother of future Taoiseach, Liam Cosgrave. The formidable Mrs. Hugh Kennedy, wife of Ireland's first Attorney General and Chief Justice, was there. So, also, was Mrs. Thomas A. Finlay, wife of the well-known barrister and TD.

Also present, at least in spirit, was St. Brigid. It was she who had inspired the recently-formed Irish Industries Purchasing League, which was established to encourage the purchase of Irish-manufactured goods. As Mr. Liam Paul, a member of the League, explained to the ladies, a preacher at the recent annual celebration of the feast of St. Brigid had spoken of the saint as "a woman who worked hard for the material benefit of the people of her country."

Prompted by this remark, "the idea came to organise the women of Ireland, the real purchasers of the wants of the home, to follow the example of St. Brigid in making work for Irish hands," Mr. Paul said. The League, he added, was "setting out to tackle the question of supporting Irish manufacture from the woman purchaser's standpoint."

With that in mind, the formidable Mrs. Kennedy proposed "that a ladies' branch of the Irish Industries Purchasing League be formed" and impressed on those present to make it their business "to ask for Irish goods, and to abuse the shops until they stocked them." Importantly, she added, it was her own experience that "if one made a fuss the shops would stock Irish goods in order not to lose a customer."

The League had identified an important issue, as Ireland, at the time, was awash with foreign-manufactured products. Wheat and flour were being imported in enormous quantities. Barley and oats were arriving in smaller amounts. Sugar, beer, whiskey and bread were also being shipped in, along with clothing and woollen goods. Ready-made suits and costumes were being manufactured on behalf of foreign multiples and sold on the main streets of Irish cities and towns.

So, also, with hosiery and boots, agricultural implements and furniture, bacon and candles, and chocolate and matches – all were arriving into Irish ports. "All of these are made in Ireland and are good of their kind, but the foreign stuff is coming in, and Irish money is going out, and men and women are vainly looking for work, and many young people when they leave school never get a chance of work at all," remarked the

National Agricultural and Industrial Development Association in mid-1931.

Many foreign products were being "dumped" on the Irish market, it was alleged. The "dumping evil," as *The Donegal Democrat* put it, was a "menace to the manufacturer and shopkeeper." With huge quantities of surplus, cut-price products thrown on the market, "the Irish industrialist or business man finds himself in a 'tight corner.' He must cut prices till he loses money, or else go out of business."

Numerous initiatives were tried or proposed by the Irish Industries Purchasing League. Public meetings and advertising campaigns were organised. "Irish Weeks" were promoted and Irish-only shop window displays arranged. School and convent heads were asked to insist on children being dressed in Irish-made clothes. The Minister for Education was lobbied to ensure lectures were provided in schools to foster the demand for Irish products.

The well-to-do proposed that "those invited to the various garden parties and other open-air functions held in Dublin during the season" should wear Irish tweed suits in an effort to promote them. How was it, one member of the League asked, that the celebrated Parisian salon of fashion designer Edward Molyneux invariably featured Irish tweeds? "If they are smart enough for Paris, surely they would be smart enough for us," she said.

It was even proposed that women might consider extending the length of their skirts. Despite the popularity of short skirts, a newspaper noted that British women had lengthened their dresses after the Prince of Wales suggested that an extra five or six inches on their length might reduce unemployment. "So great has been the effect of these few words," the newspaper remarked, "that some of the British factories are working day and night."

On a darker note, many saw that the only effective solution lay in embargos, tariffs, subsidies, and a range of other devices to protect Irish goods. "An economic policy enforced by the State is necessary to change the existing unsatisfactory conditions," the National Agricultural and Industrial Development Association argued. "We have called upon the Government to adopt that policy with steadfastness and decision."

In the end, the pro-tariff and pro-embargo lobby had its way and the days of the Irish Industries Purchasing League were numbered. The election to government of Fianna Fáil, with the support of the Labour Party, in February 1932, saw a wide range of tariffs, licenses and quotas being introduced to protect the Irish economy.

The measures resulted in the Irish Free State entering an economic war with Britain up to 1938. Many manufactured goods, including farm machinery, were subjected to tariffs and quotas. Coal imports from Britain were banned. Farmers were encouraged to turn away from the British market and concentrate on satisfying domestic demand. Almost 2,000 tariffs were in operation by 1936. The retaliation from Britain was fierce.

Coming at a time when Ireland was reeling from the crash of 1929–1932, the effects on the Irish economy were enormous. Goods were scarce, money was short, and jobs were few and far between. Guinness partially relocated to England, resulting in

500 Irish job losses. Ford, in Cork, shifted production from tractor manufacturing to car assembly, requiring fewer workers.

St. Brigid was obliged to shift her focus, too. No longer campaigning to "Buy Irish," she turned her attention to looking after those in desperate economic need. It was an undertaking that would last many years, as we can see in the following story.

St. Brigid's Penny Dinners, inspired by the saint's work in feeding the poor and hungry, was established by the Bon Secours Sisters in Dublin in 1932. It was based in an area of the city badly hit by the economic crisis taking place at the time.

Dockers living in the vicinity of Dublin's quays had a hard time during the economic crash of 1929 – 1932. Work was scarce, wages were low, and hunger was widespread. Matters weren't helped by the economic war with Britain, begun in 1932, when the Irish government's policy of protectionism and self-sufficiency further hit the area.

Workers in industrial jobs were also hit. People employed in flour milling and gas production – the other major employers – suffered badly, as did those employed in coal yards and grain stores. The area was on its knees by the time World War II was declared in 1939, bringing shortages of food, clothing and fuel.

Families struggled to survive. "I am a married man with five children," a Dubliner wrote to *The Irish Press* in February 1932, describing the parlous state of his finances. "I draw 15/- per week relief, out of which my wife pays 7/8 for rent and 1/9 society. That leaves 6/3 for food for my wife and children.

"My visiting officer says that I am forbidden to earn a few shillings selling papers on Sundays, and a few shillings on jam jars and bottles which I may pick up on the rubbish dump. The whole lot only amounts to four or five shillings per week. For trying to feed my hungry children and keep a shelter over them, my visiting officer says my relief will be stopped."

The Lord Mayor of Dublin, Alfie Byrne TD, was "gravely worried," saying "there are many heart-rending cases of whole families who are receiving no relief of any sort. It is literally starvation for many people, and the numbers of unemployed are growing in the city." There were 8,000 families living on food tickets, he added, and the courts were filled with pending evictions.

St. Brigid's Penny Dinners was established at the heart of the crisis with the aim of providing meals for hungry children and adults in the badly-affected area around Dublin's Holles Row. For a penny, adults were provided with a nourishing meal of beef and vegetable stew, a slice of bread, bread pudding, and a cup of tea or cocoa. Those who had no money were given their meals free. A special Christmas dinner was provided, with around 300 in attendance.

"Over 300 destitute men and women are daily supplied with substantial meals for the nominal charge of one penny each," a report in *The Irish Press*, in 1932, stated, "and an equal number are given to poor children by the Sisters of the Bon Secours Convent, who cook and serve the meals themselves. A special appeal is made for public support for this deserving charity."

The provision of meals for the area's hungry children proved a great, and much-needed, success. Each afternoon, at 3 o'clock, hordes of children from the local schools – City Quay School in South Gloucester Street, Loreto Convent in Leeson Lane, and St. Andrew's in Pearse Street – hurried to the centre for what, for many, would be their only nourishment of the day. Around Christmas, a special afternoon tea party was provided for the children, with some 200 in attendance.

The supply of these meals "has undoubtedly been appreciated, and there is evidence to show that children formerly found to be suffering from Malnutrition have benefited by the provision of such meals," the Department of Education noted in its annual report for 1932 – 1933. The substitution of pure whole milk for cocoa, which had been recommended by the Department, had also proved beneficial.

By the early 1950s, the pressure on St. Brigid's had grown dramatically. In 1950 alone, the centre was providing 1,000 hot meals daily to the local poor. So desperate were the pressures that the Bon Secours Sisters, in the run-up to Christmas, had to plead with newspaper readers to "make a Christmas Offering in Honour of the Infant Jesus" to support their Holles Row project. "Help us continue this work," they asked readers in anticipation of the Christmas rush.

"At this time, things were hard for families in our community," a local resident, Patrick McGauley, commented in *The New Link* magazine. "When kids got off school at 12.30 pm, they would go to the Penny Dinners on various days. You would get mince and potatoes and veg, other days you would get stew, etc.

"The best part of the meal was, as you left, you would receive a big slice of jam roll. When all the kids vanished, the older members of the community appeared, to be fed and watered. This maybe was their first and only meal of the day. Times were hard."

By the early 2000s, despite changes in its clientele, St. Brigid's was still going strong. The homeless, workers from overseas, students unable to pay their rent, and families left behind in the economic boom began to put in regular appearances. The price of a meal, a still-modest €3, had changed. The menu had changed, too, with the kitchen offering chicken soup, roast pork, two veg, and desserts of stewed apple and custard.

By that stage, the area was beyond recognition. What had once been a hive of activity and then a veritable economic wasteland had become a centre for tech companies, with office blocks, hotels, high-cost luxury apartments, car-parking spaces, and record rents. In the circumstances, "due to a change in the profile of local residents," a decision was made in 2018 to close down St. Brigid's.

There was to be an intriguing end to the story. Although the food centre was gone, the building hadn't gone with it. It soon had a new occupant. What had once attracted the poor and hungry in search of a meal was transformed into a slimming centre for people worried about the shape of their figures. Matters had certainly moved on around Holles Row!

In July 1934, for the first time in history, a national pilgrimage took place to the birthplace of St. Brigid in Faughart, County Louth. An estimated 10,000 – 15,000 people from all over Ireland gathered for the occasion.

A spell of wonderful weather prevailed in Ireland during the summer of 1934. Temperatures of up to 98° Fahrenheit were recorded in parts of the country. Bathing, boating and picnicking were much in evidence. Rainfall was negligible and reservoirs dried up. The fine weather brought good news for turf-cutters, but not for farmers, who prayed for a night's rain to bring on the crops.

The bright weather was largely welcomed by the 10,000 – 15,000 pilgrims who packed their sandwiches for the first national pilgrimage to the birthplace of St. Brigid at Faughart, County Louth. Special trains brought 3,500 people from Dublin and 1,000 from Belfast, while 100 buses and another fleet of trains brought many thousands more from all parts of the country.

For those arriving in nearby Dundalk, the scene awaiting them was spectacular. "The people of Dundalk made special efforts to beautify their town in honour of the Saint," a reporter for the *Westmeath Examiner* observed. "Pilgrims passed through the streets brightened by a display of Papal and Eucharistic Congress flags and bunting reminiscent of Dublin in June, 1932," he wrote, referring to the frenzy of colour that greeted pilgrims arriving for the famous Catholic congress held two years earlier.

Pilgrims arriving through Dundalk, or by other routes, assembled at the parish church of Kilcurry for the grand procession to St. Brigid's shrine, less than three miles distant. Decorative arches in red and white spanned parts of the route, and six bands, three of them brass, accompanied the marchers. Boy Scouts dressed in blue and Girl Guides dressed in brown were joined by several hundred confraternity members from Dublin attired in their habits.

The procession was led by the Carlingford pipers' band, followed by a horse-drawn cart containing a relic of the saint housed in a gilt casket and shrouded by a silk canopy. Girls clothed in white marched in front of the relic, while around the casket sat six girls all bearing the name Brigid. Their surnames, we are told, were Lennon, O'Hare, Marmion, Doherty, King and McMahon, all of them hailing from the district.

Behind them marched a "who's who" of Irish political life. A long line of politicians was led by Éamon de Valera, President of the Executive Council: a post signifying head of government at the time. He was accompanied by Sean T. O'Kelly, Vice-President of the Council, and W. T. Cosgrave, a former Council President. The Minister for Defence and Minster for Lands were there, as was the Ceann Comhairle, Frank Fahy.

Also present was the colourful Lord Mayor of Dublin, Alfie Byrne – known as "The Shaking Hand of Dublin" due to his perpetual proclivity for canvassing – and members of his Corporation, all of them dressed in their picturesque robes. They were being carefully monitored by the First Aid section of the Catholic Boy Scouts of Ireland, who were on the lookout for victims of the heat. They were busy that day, as more than 100 people came down with heatstroke.

"The sight as the procession wound up the hill from Kilcurry Church, whence the sacred relic was borne, was one which will never be forgotten by those who witnessed it," remarked a *Dundalk Democrat* journalist. "On the fields along the route of the procession the crowd spread for hundreds of yards, on the hillocks above the shrine they clustered. Through this vast crowd went a remarkable procession in which thousands walked..... The waiting crowds, as it broke on their view, were held silent and enthralled by it."

The two-mile-long procession took more than an hour to wind its way to St. Brigid's shrine. It was there, on the hillside, near the stream, and with a commanding view of the surrounding countryside, that the religious ceremonies were carried out. They included the "Stations of St. Brigid," Benediction and the Rosary, all broadcast to the crowd through newfangled microphones and loud speakers. It was said that during the Rosary the huge throng assembled on the hillside made the countryside ring with their responses.

There were sermons, too, with the inevitable admonishing of the less-than-faithful and calls for greater morality. "Mary of the Gael," one speaker, a priest from Waterford, preached. "What a fitting title for the purest, sweetest, most glorious of Irish womanhood. Could Brigid be proud today of her girls and her women as she had every right to be? Were they worthy to claim her, to possess her, to call her their own dear saint?

"Were they imitating her, or were they not rather imitating a moral code imported into their midst by alien, and now almost Pagan, countries? Do not our bathing places and holiday resorts, our dance halls and places of amusement give the lie to our claim to be successors of the fine ideals of Brigid, Columcille and Patrick?"

In the late afternoon of 1 July 1934, the never-to-be-forgotten spectacle at St. Brigid's shrine came to a close and the pilgrims headed for home. Thirty-one omnibuses from the Great Northern Railway's bus division ferried visitors to their trains in Dundalk. Others left by car, foot, or on the hundreds of bicycles which had been left tilted against ditches and walls near the shrine.

The pilgrimage had been a spectacular success, it was agreed, and plans were already afoot for more in the years ahead. Those dreams were realised when further national pilgrimages to the shrine took place year after year during the remainder of the 20th century and beyond. Eventually, they evolved into a "festive" celebration of the saint, deemed more appropriate to the changing times.

That first national pilgrimage in July 1934, however, would never be forgotten. Not only was it recalled as a "magnificent scene of splendour" and "difficult to equal" but it was viewed as the end of "that curious era when the Irish saints seemed to have fallen from favour in their own homeland." It was, as one newspaper headline put it, "Faughart's Day of Triumph."

Bridget Dowling, from Tallaght, County Dublin, came to prominence during World War II as the sister-in-law of Adolf Hitler.

Bridget Dowling, who later became Bridget Hitler, was born in 1891 at Kilnamanagh, near Tallaght, County Dublin. She inherited her first name from her mother, Bridget Reynolds, who in turn inherited the name from her mother, Bridget Quirke. The fact that the name was carried down through the generations was no surprise at the time.

What was surprising was that Bridget Dowling would later marry Alois Hitler – the Führer's half-brother – providing her with an entrée to the dictator's family. Although she could never have dreamt it at the time, she would end up meeting the Führer at the Berghof, his home in the Bavarian Alps.

Bridget Dowling was born into a poor, conservative Catholic family. Her father was a farm labourer who struggled to support his family. His work reflected the area the family lived in, which at the time was primarily rural, although it did have some flour and paper mills nearby. He later moved his family to a tenement in Dublin city.

In 1909, when Bridget was 18, she met the man who changed her life. They were introduced to each other at the annual Dublin Horse Show. He told her he was "Alois Hitler from Austria." She was immediately smitten. To her interested eyes, "he represented the height of elegance according to the vogue at the start of the century," she said.

The stranger, with his homburg hat, immaculate spats and debonair Viennese ways, made a big impression. "His conversation was quite different from that of the commonplace, hardworking farmers and their wives who made up the society I was accustomed to. Everything he said was so new and interesting that even his broken English seemed charming," she remarked.

Their first date was a visit to a Dublin museum in Merrion Square, followed by tea. "Need I say that I was already head over heels in love?" she said. Her parents disapproved. They might have been particularly unimpressed by the fact that Alois was employed as a waiter at the Shelbourne Hotel. The couple solved the problem by eloping to London, where they were married on 3 June 1910. They later moved to Liverpool.

On 12 March 1911 – nine months and nine days after their wedding – their only child was born in their Liverpool flat. The couple, who were practising Catholics, had the baby christened on 30 April 1911. "We had named our baby William Patrick, but it was not long before I found myself calling him Pat. Alois, however, addressed him as Willie. Both of us clung stubbornly to our chosen nicknames," she said.

Life wasn't easy for the Hitler family. "Alois had a volatile Bohemian nature and was always just about to make a fortune," Bridget noted. "He changed his way of earning a living four times during our first two years of married life." He first opened a small restaurant, then opened a boarding house, followed by a hotel, and then went bankrupt. "There were times I didn't have enough money to buy milk for my baby," Bridget remarked.

Alois next got involved in a razor business, which also failed. He then announced that he was departing for Germany, from where he planned to launch an English razor on the Continental market. He wrote occasionally, his last card postmarked Berlin on 28 July 1914. That card marked the end of their marriage.

Fifteen years later, in 1929, William Patrick, then aged 18, travelled to Germany at the request of his father. By that stage, Alois had married again and had another child, named Heinz. The family were living in Berlin. The following year, 1930, he visited once more and met his "Uncle Adolf." They indulged in coffee, whipped cream and homemade cake. They also discussed religion.

With the Führer's help, William Patrick eventually got a job with the Reichskreditbank, followed by employment with the Opel car company. Eventually, his wild social life and proclivity for talking about his famous uncle incurred Adolf's wrath. "I didn't become Chancellor for the benefit of my family.....No one is going to climb on my back," Hitler reputedly remarked.

In public, he referred to William Patrick as "my loathsome nephew."

In 1937, Bridget travelled to Berlin, where she met Alois at his fashionable restaurant not far from the Chancellery. She met her brother-in-law, Adolf, as well. She was invited to his home at Berchtesgaden, in the Bavarian Alps. There they ate scrambled eggs, asparagus swimming in butter, artichokes, mushrooms, salad and dessert.

Hitler was charming and called her Brigette. "It is difficult to deceive a woman; she can always tell when a man is posing. Adolf was a born actor, who played even for a one-person audience," she later noted. They, too, talked about religion. "When I have my say, Catholicism's days will be numbered," she reported him as saying.

On her return to England, Bridget was hounded by the press. Newspapers carried headlines featuring "Mrs. Bridget Hitler," "Dictator's Sister-in-Law," "Sister-in-Law of Hitler," "Fuehrer's Irish-born Sister-in-Law," or just plain "Mrs. Hitler." In an interview with the *Daily Express*, she said: "Nowadays it's a bit embarrassing to be Mrs. Hitler, but the people who know me don't mind, and the others don't matter. At heart, I'm still Bridget Dowling."

In 1939, Bridget accompanied her son on a speaking tour of the United States, and they remained there for the rest of their lives. They settled in New York, where they changed their name from Hitler to Stuart-Houston. While there, Bridget wrote a memoir which claimed that Adolf Hitler had, in 1912, come to stay with her and Alois in Liverpool. Historians have cast doubt on the claim.

Bridget Hitler died in 1969 at the age of 78, and her son, William Patrick, passed away in 1987 aged 76. They are buried beside each other at the Holy Sepulchre Cemetery in Coram, Long Island, New York. On the gravestone, Bridget's name is engraved "Brigid Elisabeth," an erroneous spelling of the name she acquired at birth. There is no mention of the name she acquired through marriage – Bridget Hitler!

In April 1946, an Irish-born war bride, Bridget McCluskey, travelled to America to get justice for herself and her baby. What followed propelled the name "Bridget" on to the front pages of the American press.

During World War II – in March 1944 – a pretty, 24-year-old, Irish-born nurse, Bridget Mary McCluskey, travelled to London on leave from her job at a Liverpool hospital. While there, she met a 36-year-old man named Frank Knowlton Waters, an American from California who was working as a technician for an aircraft company.

They had a passionate affair and were married within weeks. There was nothing unusual about that as instant marriages between local women and American men, especially GIs, were common. Although Frank was no GI, he had a good job and was planning to develop his career back in the States. Bridget could hardly wait.

Following the war, business took Frank to France, but Bridget was prevented from accompanying him due to post-war restrictions. The next Bridget heard from him was in a letter, where he explained that "the marriage was a mistake." He said he didn't intend to live with her again. He was, he told her, leaving for America – alone!

Bridget, who was pregnant, was distraught. Frank, her son, was born soon after. His father promised child support of $50 a month, but he never paid a penny. What's more, she soon learned that he was suing her for divorce. "He can't do that! I won't let him!" she said.

Bridget contacted the British Married Women's Association, whose advisors persuaded her to become the first British war wife to contest the divorce action of an American husband. Backed by the association, she secured a visitor's visa to the United States. She arrived there on 13 April 1946.

Reporters came out in force to meet her. "I'm the first British war bride to arrive here to contest a husband's divorce action," she told them. "There will be a lot more coming. There are a lot of brides getting divorce papers in the mail these days and not all of them will take it sitting down."

The press noted that Bridget seemed conflicted. One minute she was saying, "Frank says he made a mistake! Well, if he made a mistake he is bloody well about to pay for it!" The next minute she was saying, "I love him!" One reporter suggested she should call Frank, which she did. He agreed to meet her in Las Vegas, where he was working in a bank.

The couple eventually met at Boulder City, which is about 26 miles south-east of Las Vegas. There, Frank saw his son for the first time. He fell in love with him. Unfortunately, there was no rekindling of affection for "Beasie," which was the nickname she carried with her from Ireland. He was going ahead with the divorce, he said.

The divorce case was heard on 27 April by District Judge A. S. Henderson and a jury. Bridget told her story in quiet tones. The jury glared at Frank as she did so. Not only did they throw out his divorce petition, but they awarded Bridget $100 a month in support, with a back payment of $1,000 added in for good measure.

Frank was now stuck in his "marriage" with Bridget, and Bridget was stuck in Las Vegas as she feared that Frank would never pay her a penny if she returned to England or Ireland. She found a home for herself and her baby in the house of a Mr. and Mrs. C. W. Biggs. She also found work at the Clark County General Hospital in Las Vegas.

Frank often came to see his son and took Bridget – once – on an outing to Mount Charleston, a nearby summer resort. He even introduced her to his mother who, she later said, treated her "like an unwelcome stranger."

Perhaps Bridget hoped that a reconciliation between the couple might take place, but those hopes were dashed when Frank told her he still wanted a divorce. He also told her he wanted custody of their child.

She then discovered that he was seeing another woman and hired private detectives to follow him. She also borrowed a .22 calibre revolver from the wife of a Las Vegas casino bouncer, saying she "feared prowlers."

The weather in Las Vegas on the afternoon of Labor Day, 2 September 1946, was warm, partly cloudy, with no rain forecast. Frank Knowlton Waters arrived at the Biggs' home to take his son on an outing. His landlady was with him, sitting in her car in front of the house.

Suddenly, the landlady heard a shot. She also saw Bridget running from the house, screaming "I've just killed him!" When the police arrived they found Frank lying on the floor of the Biggs' living room. He had been shot through the heart. The bullet that killed him had grazed the baby's right leg.

Bridget, who was hysterical, was imprisoned in the Las Vegas gaol. There, she explained what had happened. She had learned, she said, that Frank was having an affair with his landlady's daughter, Lucille, who was divorced and the mother of three children. When he arrived that day at her lodgings, she had brought up Lucille's name in their conversation.

"Where did you hear about her?" Frank asked. "I heard about her ten days ago and I haven't slept since," she replied. "Is it because of her that you want a divorce?" she asked. "Yes," he answered. As they spoke, he looked "vicious and frightening," she commented.

Frank took a step towards her and she fled to the bedroom to get the gun. When she returned, he was holding little Frank. "Don't you dare touch the baby," she screamed. The look on his face was "dangerous," she remarked. He said: "I'm taking the baby where you won't see him again."

With the gun in her left hand, she reached for the baby with her right hand, Bridget said. Frank tried to grab the gun and it went off. "I didn't intend to kill him," she stated. "I just wanted to get him out of the house."

On 20 October 1946, Bridget's trial opened in Las Vegas to a fanfare of publicity. The opening day was dramatic. "Nevada has never executed a woman and I don't aim to start such a precedent now," the District Attorney announced to the jury.

"But this woman shot her husband in cold blood, with no provocation." Bridget shrieked: "It is not so! It is not so!"

Once calm was restored, the trial continued. The proceedings were long and complicated, involving many witnesses and reams of evidence. Eventually, the jurors retired to discuss their verdict. For 19 hours they wrangled. Three jurors wanted to convict Bridget of second degree murder; the others took varying views. Compromising, they found her guilty of involuntary manslaughter.

On 6 November, "the Irish widow," as she was called in the press, was sent to Carson City state penitentiary to serve a one to five-year term of imprisonment. She faced deportation on her release, as stipulated by the jury. "I am satisfied with the verdict," she said. In the interim, her son was sent to a children's home in Reno.

"Irish Slayer of Hubby 'Happy' to Sail Home" was the headline in New York's *Daily News* on 3 June 1948. The report concerned Bridget. The previous day, having served 18 months of her sentence, she and her three-year-old son had been deported to England on board the *Marine Flasher*.

On the day of her departure, we are told, she wore a green cloth coat, white print dress, white shoes and a single string of pearls. She smiled off and on for reporters and looked at ease. When asked if she still thought about the killing, she said: "I don't think about it at all." Asked if she was sorry for having killed her husband, she declined to reply.

Bridget then stepped aboard the boat, which was berthed at Pier 90, North River, in New York's docks, and placed her three-year-old in his cot in their cabin. She then returned to the deck and watched New York recede into the fading distance. Apart from interviews she gave to reporters on her arrival in England, she was never heard from again.

Places of detention known as "Bridewells" were once present in numerous Irish cities and towns. The name was derived from the Irish saint.

Author and playwright Brendan Behan knew a thing or two about Bridewells. In 1942, the IRA recruit was detained in the Bridewell, Dublin, prior to being sentenced to 14 years for attempted murder and possession of firearms. A few years earlier, he had been detained in Dale Street Bridewell, Liverpool, before being sentenced to three years in borstal for possession of explosives.

The Dublin Bridewell at least had "a proper 'jacks' in the corner," he later said, so he didn't have to slop out his cell. The cleaners in Dublin were also more compassionate. On hearing that he was in for shooting at the police, one of them remarked, almost in tears: "Jesus, Mary and Joseph, God help your poor mother." "Screw my mother," Behan responded. "It's not her they'll be hanging, it's me."

Behan was well aware that the institutions he frequented owed their name to St. Brigid, the Irish saint. The name had originated in an area of London, just off Fleet Street, which incorporated Bride Lane and St. Bride's Church, the steeple of which had inspired the tiered wedding cake featured earlier in this book. More importantly, it also had a holy well, St. Bride's Well, whose name was eventually abbreviated to "Bridewell."

Did Londoners ever wonder about the origin of those names? Behan reflected. Did they ever ask how the "church of Saint Bride," as he called it, came into existence? "How many of the thousands of Londoners, to whom these names are familiar, give thought to the common Celtic heritage of these islands from the days of antiquity?" he asked in his autobiography, *Confessions of an Irish Rebel*.

Behan, it seems, knew his history. The earliest indications are that a well existed in the area as far back as Roman times. Later, in the sixth century, a growing Celtic-Christian community dedicated the well to St. Brigid, believing it was she who was responsible for its special properties. From then on, it was known as St. Bride's Well.

The first Bridewell – a large, imposing building using the abbreviated name – was built in the area by Cardinal Wolsey and eventually used as a royal palace. Having housed people like Henry VIII, in time it fell into disuse and disrepair. With royal consent, it then became a hospital, orphanage and prison. It was eventually used as a short-term facility for petty offenders, vagabonds and "loose women."

Although bearing St. Brigid's name, its reputation for inflicting grisly punishments was far from saintly. Records describe how a woman was sentenced to be "whipped at Bridewell" and afterwards "placed in the pillory in Cheapside with a paper in her hand, whereon was written – 'Whipped at Bridewell for leaving and forsaking her child in the streets.'" Although severe, her punishment was much milder than the tortures inflicted on others.

Soon, places of detention throughout Britain and Ireland were being called Bridewells, and the name spread far and wide. By the mid-19th century, in excess of 100 were located in Irish cities and towns. In 1844, for example, they could be found anywhere from Dingle in County Kerry to Ballymena in County Antrim, and from Enniscorthy in County Wexford to Buncrana in County Donegal.

One Irish Bridewell – the Richmond in Dublin – once held the nationalist leader Daniel O'Connell for a period of three months. Reports indicate that he was treated well and housed in the Governor's private quarters. Conditions were less comfortable for other inmates, who faced floggings, solitary confinement and punishment on the treadmill. The Richmond Bridewell was eventually closed and now houses Griffith College.

Another Bridewell – this one in Cork – featured prominently during the 1870 tailors' riots, when working tailors, and others, took to the streets demanding better wages. The Bridewell was attacked and an attempt was made to storm it. A company of infantry and a troop of cavalry were called in to contain the crowd. The "Irish hobbledehoy" and the "Irish rough", with his love for fighting, including returned "Americanised natives," were responsible for the "disgraceful proceedings," *The Daily News* stridently declared.

As the 1870s progressed, government policy concerning Bridewells changed and a decision was taken to phase them out. In 1878 alone, it was announced that 50 Bridewells in counties Kerry, Clare, Sligo, Donegal, Galway, Mayo, Meath, Tipperary, Waterford, Wexford and Wicklow, among others, "shall be no longer needed for the detention of prisoners."

Instead, prisoners would be transported either to county gaols or centralised prisons. Apart from two – one in Dublin, the other in Cork – Bridewells became a relic of the past.

St. Bride's Well in London also came to an end. Its demise is dated to July 1821 by the early 19th-century English author and bookseller, William Hone. The cause, he explained, was the coronation of King George IV at Westminster, which prompted the filling of thousands of bottles of water in the few days before the event. The well, as a result, dried up, the only indicator of its existence being an old cast-iron pump that survived in Bride Lane.

St. Bride's Well may have disappeared, but its legacy lived on. As another author of the era, Alfred James Copeland, reminds us, it had given its name to a street, church, palace, hospital and prison. Of course, it had also given its name "to almost every house of correction throughout the kingdom," as Copeland remarked, reminding us of those dark, grubby, wretched places of detention that once graced every town and city of substance in Great Britain and Ireland.

In 1958 – the same year Brendan Behan's newly-published book *Borstal Boy* was banned in Ireland – a Donegal man reminisced about St. Brigid's feast day in times gone by. The story, concerning the Donegal Gaeltacht, was published in a number of local newspapers.

For people living in the Donegal Gaeltacht, the first day of February was eagerly anticipated. Snowbound, stormy, cloud-covered, dreary times were coming to an end and would soon be replaced by the warmth of spring. A fresh spirit entered people's veins. From then on, people could see the lengthening of the day and the beginning of a new season's growth.

For Gaeltacht children, St. Brigid's Day brought the first respite from the gloom that followed Christmas. "Currant-cake, shop-bread, biscuits, jams and fruit were practically unobtainable in our valley except at Christmas and on big occasions. They were reserved for and sampled only on feast-days. Hence our looking forward with such eager avidity to St. Brigid's Day," the Donegal author reflected on his Gaeltacht childhood in the early 1900s.

"After school on the 31st of January, around fifty years ago, we would set out with breadknife and scissors and maybe a hook down to a low-lying holm by the Gweebarra," the anonymous man, who lived near the Gweebarra River in Donegal, wrote in 1958. "Here groves of green rushes grow in plentiful profusion, much to our joy but to our parents' dismay (for the land was almost at water level)."

A sheaf of rushes was borne home triumphantly and placed against the gable wall. When the supper was prepared, the eldest girl of the family carried the sheaf to the front door and, in Irish, called aloud: "Go on your knees, open your eyes and let in Brigid." To this exhortation the household, kneeling, would reply, again in Irish: "She is welcome, she is welcome, the lady is welcome." The procedure was repeated at the back door, and once again at the front door but this time the response was: "Blessed Brigid is welcome."

The sheaf of rushes was then deposited under the table and the family settled down to supper. When the feasting was finished, "many a long Gaelic prayer of gratitude and supplication" was offered up devoutly, "plus a remembrance of all those of seven successive generations who had passed away in our old hillside homestead." The family then settled in around the fire, where the work began.

"Around the blazing turf hearth-fire we each made or learned to make those picturesque rush criss-crosses so characteristic of the Donegal Gaeltacht," the man recalled. Rushes were bent, cross-joined, and shaped into the traditional form of St. Brigid's Crosses. Sometimes, golden wheat or oat straws were used alternatively with green rushes, producing a pleasing contrast. Not uncommonly, the work continued until two o'clock, when the family retired to bed.

At some stage before retiring, a piece of cloth, perhaps a cap, scarf, shawl or blouse, was placed outside in a basket or on a bush. There it remained until the following morning when it was retrieved, having been "blessed by Brigid." The cloth, known as a "Brat Bhríde" (Brigid's mantle), was claimed to bring many cures to people and animals. It was often worn for safety by fishermen or those undertaking long land journeys.

"On the morning of St. Brigid's Day all these crossogs and other cruciform creations are sprinkled with Holy Water before being pinned-up in kitchen, rooms, byre and outhouses – for good luck and protection from evil during the coming year," the man wrote. Normally, they were hung in every room of the house and in outhouses as a shield against sickness and disease.

A few of the remaining rushes were tied around the head to avert headaches. In one part of the Donegal Gaeltacht, these loose rushes were tied around the head, arms and legs and, following the family Rosary, were placed in the fire. If they burned out completely it was taken for granted that people living in the house would be alive and well the following year.

"Lovers' headaches" were also catered for, he remarked. Last year's cross was placed on the fire as a marriage omen: "If it merely smoulders, the affaire-de-coeur will fizzle out – but if it burns brightly, it will be a 'go!'"

Referring to other miraculous outcomes, the man recalled an event in Dungloe in the late 1890s. It was the closing night of the three-week-long, first-ever "Big Mission" in the town. "The church was so crowded that the then one-and-only gallery was heard to creak and seemed to be sagging," he recollected. A catastrophe appeared imminent.

"There was an old woman from the Hills sitting at the altar rails. In the near-panic excitement she jumped up and pulled off her Brat Bhríde blouse and waved it fervently in full faith and confidence towards the gallery," he recalled. She prayed aloud, once again in Irish: "Brigid's Mantle, protect you who are so near the abyss of disaster!" The gallery slowly emptied, the peril was averted, and the ceremonies were concluded in the chapel yard. The danger had been avoided "suspiciously," he said.

"Those were the good old days of firm faith and simple belief more than a century ago," the man reflected in 1958. It was a time "before television or atom fission were dreamt of, when neither radio or radar was known and even the motor-car and gramophone were seldom seen or heard." Great, wonderful days they were, he concluded, when "the tedium of snow-bound, cloud-cowled winter" was brought to a close by the arrival of St. Brigid's Eve and St. Brigid's Day in the Gaeltacht areas of Donegal.

Brigitte – the French version of Brigid or Bridget – became the most popular girls' name in France in 1959. It was propelled there by the rise to fame of the iconic film star, Brigitte Bardot.

Brigitte Bardot's Catholic parents chose an unusual name for their daughter at the time of her birth in September 1934. Although deeply committed to their faith, her father, Louis, and mother, Anne-Marie, decided against the most popular girls' name in France at the time – the resoundingly-Catholic Marie.

Nor did they opt for the other fashionable names of the era – Jacqueline, Monique, Jeannine, Denise or Yvette. Instead, they chose Brigitte, which in 1934 did not even feature in the top 100 girls' names in France. It was a fateful move by the parents, as the name eventually rose to international prominence thanks to their extraordinary daughter.

The name had arrived in France in many ways. Not long after St. Brigid's death, Irish missionaries and emigrants had brought it to many parts of the country. They particularly brought it to Brittany, where numerous churches were dedicated to the Irish saint.

It had also arrived indirectly, via Sweden, where one of its queens, Birgitta Haraldsdotter, had an Irish grandmother, Brigida O'Brien. The queen popularised the name in Sweden. Later on, a bearer of the name, St. Birgitta of Sweden, became popular throughout Europe, including in France.

By the age of 15, the stunningly-beautiful Brigitte Bardot – who as a young schoolgirl had worn steel-rimmed glasses and a brace on her teeth – was modelling on the cover of *Elle*, the acclaimed French lifestyle magazine for women. At the time, she lived in Paris with her wealthy, conservative parents, who adhered to Catholicism and ensured that their daughter was brought up in the practices and traditions of the Catholic faith.

Brigitte was raised in the affluent Rue de la Pompe, a stone's throw from the Eiffel Tower. Her school, Cours Hattemer, included among its students prominent Catholics such as future French President Jacques Chirac and Prince Rainier of Monaco. She also received her First Communion, attended church and catechism class, and paid regular visits to the nuns.

"Ten years later," as Irish journalist Mary Kenny put it, "she was a steamy sex-symbol who drove men crazy and elicited hate-mail from women who accused her – probably with justification – of having debauched their husbands just by her pictures." By then, she had progressed from fashion model to film star and had aroused international attention by her extraordinary good looks and her devil-may-care attitude and live-now, pay-later approach to life.

Among her mid-1950s films was the controversial *And God Created Woman*, in which Brigitte played an orphan girl with a high level of sexual energy. It was banned in many parts of America, where it was deemed to be "lewd, lascivious and immoral." Catholics there were advised by the National Legion of Decency against attending showings. Despite being condemned, it ran for more than six months in New York.

In Ireland, it took more than a decade before the film was deemed acceptable for viewing by audiences, and when it did appear it was restricted to "adults only." The same fate befell other Bardot films, such as *Mam'selle Striptease* – abbreviated to *Mam'selle* in Ireland – in which the lead was played by the "lovely

Brigitte," according to Cork's *Evening Echo*. "Although the censor had to use his scissors here, it did not spoil the continuity of the picture," the newspaper noted.

"She heralded the sexual revolution which was to happen in the 1960s in a way that was bound to scandalise the bourgeoisie," Bardot's biographer, Glenys Roberts, wrote in 1984 of the star's image as a sultry, sensual sex kitten. "It was not just that she was a very beautiful woman. It was that she symbolised the permissive revolution which was on the way. People sensed that. They knew she was dangerous."

That sense of danger was highlighted in December 1952 when, aged 18, Bardot topped off an almost three-year affair by marrying film director, Roger Vadim. Despite her unconventional, free-spirited reputation, the wedding was held at Notre-Dame de Grâce de Passy Catholic church in Paris, not far from her home. It was a proper church wedding, for which Vadim prepared with twice-a-week catechism lessons.

The marriage subsequently failed and the couple divorced in 1957. Although she later went on to have numerous high-profile affairs and was married four times, she still retained her religious convictions, but with qualifications. Describing herself as "a great believer," she clarified her views in her autobiography *Tears of Battle: An Animal Rights Memoir*.

"I hold the idea of religion and its hierarchy at a distance," she remarked in the book. "The 'ministers of God' I met were often disappointing, apart from rare exceptions.....Religion always makes me think of immobility. Its structures do not change, and the people in those structures seem static."

Among the religious figures she respected was Pope John Paul II, who she met during an audience in 1995. By then, Brigitte was a well-known animal activist, campaigning in their defence and fighting for their protection and rights. "I felt something powerful pass between us," she later recalled. The meeting, she remarked, was "an unforgettable experience."

Three other religious figures continued to dominate her life. The first was St. Francis of Assisi, whose love of animals she admired and whose simplicity she emulated. On reading of his life, she was struck by his decision to relinquish material possessions. Inspired by his example, she sold at auction her most precious belongings and used the funds for her Brigitte Bardot Foundation, which provides for the welfare and protection of animals.

The second religious figure she remained close to was the Virgin Mary. "She and I have a very close bond," Brigitte remarked in her book. "Now I go to meet her whenever I feel like it, the way I would with a dear friend or a mother. I speak to her frankly.....sometimes I don't say anything at all; I speak to her with my heart.....I confide in her about my pains, my joys, my hopes, and my passions."

Lastly, she retained affection for her saintly namesake, who remained prominent in her life. Many of Bardot's important turning points were linked to her. But the debt worked two ways. After all, it was the film star who, back in the 1950s, edged the saint's name past Sylvie, Marie, Martine, Françoise and Dominique until in 1959 it finally rose to the top of the charts to become, at least for that year, the most popular girls' name in France.

The decision by Telefís Éireann in 1961 to adopt the St. Brigid's Cross as the symbol of the new station was inspired by one of its managers, Edith Cusack, whose life story was tragic, to say the least.

Dense fog blanketed England on the evening of 22 November 1948. Visibility was reduced to zero in many parts of the country. Three airports were closed, trains were cancelled, and cars had to slow to a crawl. The conditions in some areas were described as "the worst within memory."

Shortly after dark, residents of the tiny parish of Chute, in South-West England, were startled by the roar of a plane which was clearly in trouble. Within seconds, it crashed, ploughed up lawns, skidded towards a copse, and burst into flames.

Villagers arriving at the scene were shocked by the carnage they encountered. Seven airmen lay dead in the burning remains of their Lancaster aircraft. One crewman – a radio officer – had been thrown clear and survived the crash. Badly burned, he was rushed to hospital.

Among the dead was Captain William Cusack, aged 25, from Limerick. A former captain with Aer Lingus, he had earlier served in the RAF. On that night in 1948, he and his colleagues were returning from Germany where they had been involved in the Berlin Airlift.

At the time, Captain Cusack was employed by a company called Flight Refuelling Ltd., which was ferrying fuel to beleaguered Berlin residents. Caught up in the Soviet Union's blockade of the Allied-controlled sector of the city, the population were desperate for supplies. Among those helping to provide relief was the young Irish airman.

Seventeen months earlier, Captain Cusack had married a young, strikingly-attractive woman named Edith Newman. Not only was Edith well known as a model, but she had also risen to Chief Air Hostess with Aer Lingus. The wedding ceremony was performed by her brother, an RAF chaplain. Best man was Aer Lingus Captain Aidan Quigley, who would later ferry Pope John Paul II to Ireland.

Following her husband's death, Edith returned to work at Aer Lingus. To begin with, she took charge of the Booking Office and was later appointed Passenger Relations Officer. She also studied for a diploma in public relations, which she successfully completed. Allied to her modelling work and part-time teaching at the College of Commerce, Dublin – where her job was to turn "girls" into "perfect secretaries" – she was certainly busy.

Life, however, was lonely without her husband. "I like a real family Christmas," she remarked in the lead-up to one festive season. "My six brothers and two sisters go to Midnight Mass and then to early Mass on Christmas Day with their children. I have no children, but I always go along, too." On that Christmas Day she was planning to spend time with her brother and family at his home in a Dublin suburb.

In 1961, Edith applied for and was appointed to the post of Head of Women's Programmes at the soon-to-be-launched Telefís Éireann. Speaking of her new job, she said: "I have been in contact with women of all nationalities all along and with women's associations. I think I know what they want. I have a clear mind, and with an amount of consultation, I think I should be able to cater for women all over the country."

Inspired by the use of the shamrock at Aer Lingus, Edith proposed to her new employer that the St. Brigid's Cross might be an appropriate emblem for the fledgling station. Her suggestion, made soon after her appointment, was accepted. Within weeks, Eamonn Andrews, Chairman of the Irish Broadcasting Authority, was announcing the decision.

"We hope Irish television will spread its cloak as effectively as St. Brigid did hers," Andrews said at a launch of the emblem in Gormanston, County Meath. "She was an intellectual dairy-maid, a cow-hand with culture, a field labourer who promoted art and literature. Please God, we cow-hands and labourers of Irish television will do half as much, twice as quickly."

On Tuesday, 5 September 1961, the first Irish television test transmission – the St. Brigid's Cross – flashed up on television sets in areas of the country covered by the Kippure transmitter. From then on, from 3 pm to 5 pm, five days a week, test-card signals, accompanied by soft Irish music, were transmitted so that TV dealers and set owners could make the necessary adjustments on their receivers to ensure a good picture.

Then, on New Year's Eve 1961, the St. Brigid's Cross put in another historic appearance, before vanishing from TV screens at the precise stroke of 7 pm. At that moment, the cross was replaced by an Irish Army lieutenant hoisting the national colours. The strains of a specially-arranged version of the National Anthem were interspersed with scenes of Irish life, followed by a speech from President Éamon de Valera. Thus was born Ireland's new television service – Telefís Éireann.

For the best part of the next two years, Edith Cusack performed her work as Head of Women's Programmes with

Ireland's new broadcaster. The three programmes she managed reflected her personal interests and sense of style. One of those programmes, *Face Facts*, which was presented by beautician Bronwyn Conroy, provided women with "useful hints about beauty care."

Another programme, *My Job and I*, featured women including air hostesses, rail hostesses, commercial artists and one TD describing their work. The third, *Invitation*, was a magazine programme covering "urgent, unusual and interesting" issues of relevance to women.

Although she appeared to enjoy her job, in September 1963 – little more than two years after joining the station – Edith revealed that she was departing Telefís Éireann. The shock announcement made front-page news. "She will be getting married early next month in New York," the *Irish Independent* revealed. "Her late husband, a pilot, lost his life in the Berlin Airlift," the newspaper added.

Edith lived in the USA for a time along with her new husband, Joseph Karney. While there, she worked at several jobs including social secretary to Mrs. Heinz of the world-famous food processing firm. Eventually, the couple returned to Ireland, where they were based in Dun Laoghaire, County Dublin.

Tragically, Edith didn't have long to live. In 1971, just eight years after she had left Telefís Éireann, she died in Dublin. Press obituaries noted her diverse career – her time as a model, air hostess, broadcast manager, and widow of the tragic Captain Cusack who had predeceased her in 1948.

But the press also noted another contribution she had made in her brief broadcasting career. "It was her suggestion that St.

Brigid's Cross be used as the station symbol," *The Cork Examiner* recalled in their tribute to this remarkable woman. The initiative may have been a footnote to her life, but it was an important one, nevertheless.

The phrase "old biddy" comes from Biddy, a derivative of the name Brigid. Old biddies were often troublesome to have around, as viewers of the 1960s and '70s TV series *The Riordans* knew all too well.

The stereotypical "old biddy" may best be defined as a gossipy, interfering, often fussy woman, who is normally elderly although not always so. She is the type of woman who knows everyone's business, who peeps through her curtains to ascertain what's going on, and who is happy to share her information with others.

The classic old biddy was Minnie Brennan, the gossip and busybody of *The Riordans*, which was broadcast by Telefís Éireann from 1965 – 1979. She was the scourge of Leestown, with an unnatural ability to gather intelligence concerning her neighbours, and to know about their financial and amorous affairs.

Dressed in her tea-cosy hat and fully-buttoned heavy coat, while wearing unfashionable glasses and a scarf, she looked every inch the village gossip. That the actress who played her – Annie D'Alton – had been born in Bridewell Lane, Carlow, and was educated at the Brigidine Convent boarding school, Tullow, was ironic as she would become famous for something else associated with St. Brigid – being an "old biddy."

Where the phrase came from is interesting. St. Brigid's name was abbreviated to Biddy, which in turn gave rise to "old biddy" in the late 18th century. It became a pejorative phrase thanks to older house servants named Biddy who knew too much. They knew more about their mistresses than their masters did, and vice versa. They were happy to share their knowledge below stairs or, if they were in the mood, with all and sundry. It wasn't the best of recipes for being popular, hence their toxic reputation.

"Minnie Brennan was the archetypal old local busybody, who was beautifully positioned in the post office and who knew everything that was going on in the town," Wesley Burrowes, chief scriptwriter of *The Riordans*, explained to the authors of this book shortly before he died. She also ran Minnie Brennan's Home Bakery. No one was better placed to sniff out the smallest signs of something unfamiliar in a place like Leestown.

As with many Irish towns and villages, Leestown's residents had become intimately known to each other over the years. People were so unchanged in their ways that even the slightest deviation from the norm would be noticed. "A pair of new curtains in a front room, a coat of fresh lime on a gable, a car from Dublin, a strange priest, none of these can hope to pass unnoticed," Burrowes once remarked in an article in the *Irish Farmers' Journal*. Minnie would be on to these nuances in a flash.

Like lots of gossips she didn't always get things right. Getting the phone installed almost proved her downfall. "There'll be none of us safe now," one of the soap's characters said on hearing the news. "What does she want with a phone? Hasn't she radar already?" said another. Even the doctor was worried, since Minnie could now describe her symptoms to him at any time of day or night.

Her first attempted phone call had explosive results. She went into the shop, located the new directory and found the Riordans' number. On dialling the phone, something strange happened, as it often did in those days. She heard a click. Then she heard the voice of Benjy Riordan, who was married to Maggie. Surprisingly, he was talking to Delia, the sister of Eamon Maher, a settled Traveller.

".....this is the only way we can do it, Delia," she heard him say in mid-sentence. She thought of putting the phone down but something deep in her nature stopped her from doing so. Then she heard Benjy saying, ".....will you be able to steal out tonight?" "If I can, but if I don't come at the time, don't wait," Delia replied. "I'll wait till the crack of dawn anyway," said Benjy.

Minnie was shocked and confused. It was "as if she had somehow been caught listening," as Burrowes explained, and she put the phone down. She assumed the worst, not realising that Benjy and Delia had been rehearsing lines for a play, *Sive*, by John B. Keane. She decided to take action and was soon spreading rumours in the hope of discouraging what she thought to be a flourishing love affair. Her intervention, unfortunately, created a tangled mess.

Everyone knew what she was at. Minnie began to regret her actions. In depressed mood, she went to Fr. Sheehy looking for help. Years before, she had worked for him as his housekeeper. On this occasion, Miss O'Callaghan, Fr. Sheehy's present housekeeper and a decent woman, let her in.

Ordinarily, Minnie would have engaged in conversation and shared some gossip. Indeed, she might have launched into a few sarcastic remarks about an ornament not dusted or a dirty window, something that would "never have happened" in her day. But today, she was too depressed for that.

"Good morning," Miss O'Callaghan said. "Good morning," Minnie replied meekly. Miss O'Callaghan noticed the black mood. "Minnie Brennan's waiting for you in the parlour, Father," she said, having gone to fetch the priest. "What does she want?" he asked. "She didn't say. I think she's not well," the housekeeper responded. "She didn't say anything?" he queried in a highly-puzzled manner. "Not a word," Miss O'Callaghan replied. "Then she can't be well," Fr. Sheehy responded with some gravity.

During their conversation, Minnie revealed all about her gossiping. Fr. Sheehy was supportive and forgiving. One thing puzzled him, though, and that was how Minnie had believed there was an extramarital affair in the first place. It was the phone call, Minnie explained, and she started outlining the details of what was said.

"There was something he said that sounded funny," Minnie remarked regarding the words spoken by Benjy. "I mean it wasn't like Benjy Riordan to say it – oh, I have it. He said he'd wait for her till the crack of dawn. Wasn't that peculiar now, Father? Benjy Riordan waiting any place till the crack of dawn and him with the milking to face."

Suddenly, the light dawned on Fr. Sheehy, who was the play's producer. While walking her to the door, he asked: "Are you coming to the play, Minnie?" "I suppose I am, Father, I hadn't thought.....” She was thinking that Fr. Sheehy had chosen a very odd moment to sell tickets. “Here you are then, Minnie, with my compliments,” he said, fishing a ticket out of his pocket. “You’ll be sure to come now – I think you’ll get something out of it!”

We all know a Minnie Brennan, “a next-door neighbour, a woman down the road, a local shopkeeper, bubbling over with the latest gossip and rumour,” wrote Fr. Morgan Costello, a curate, in the *Evening Herald*, in 1972. “They add a bit of colour to life and a lot of confusion. They cannot understand why people object to their activities. They mean so well!”

Minnie Brennan, he pointed out, was the best example you could find. She brightened our Sunday evenings. Life was never dull when she was around. She kept us informed about Benjy and Maggie, and other bits of spicy news from Leestown. “But while we smile at her antics,” he concluded that we are grateful that the old biddy “lives in Leestown and not next door.”

Minnie’s gossiping came to an end in 1979 when the TV series, *The Riordans*, was axed by Telefís Éireann. Actress Annie D’Alton was shocked when she heard the news that her famous character would be no more. “It’s terrible, terrible,” the woman who had brought the term “Mary Dear” into the nation’s vocabulary remarked. “What will the people do on Sunday nights without the news and the gossip from Leestown?”

It was bad enough that her job was gone, she concluded, but what was even worse was the way she heard the news. It came as a result of a phone call from a journalist. For once, the old biddy, Minnie, was not the first with the news!

St. Brigid became well known to Aer Lingus customers following the end of World War II. Since then, her name has graced many of its planes.

At ten minutes past nine, on the morning of 15 June 1967, Jacqueline Kennedy and her two children, Caroline and John, arrived at Shannon Airport on board the *St. Brigid* from New York. The early-morning mists were clearing as Flight 104 touched down and taxied to the terminal building. On what promised to be a warm, sun-drenched day, a large crowd waited to welcome the glamorous former First Lady to Ireland.

Jacqueline emerged through the door of the *St. Brigid*'s first-class section – the Golden Shamrock compartment – dressed in a semi-fitted powder blue mini-coat and wearing her trademark shoulder-length bouffant hairstyle. The crowd, estimated to be in the thousands, greeted her with resounding applause. Obviously touched by the welcome, the "petite and beautiful young woman," as one newspaper described her, addressed the well-wishers.

"I am so happy to be here in this land which my husband loved so much," she said. "For myself and the children it's a little bit like coming home, and we're looking forward to it dearly." She was referring to the private five-week holiday which she and some family friends had planned to spend at Woodstown House, seven miles from Waterford city. The ceremonies over, she left the crowd and the *St. Brigid* behind her and headed to her holiday destination.

The national airline's policy of naming its planes after saints was initiated after World War II. The objective was simple: to combine powerful symbols of Irish modernisation – the company's fleet of planes – with older, distinctly Catholic symbols from

Irish history. That combination, it was believed, would go down particularly well in the North American market.

St. Patrick, St. Brigid and St. Columcille were the obvious names that came to mind. Soon, there was a much longer list of candidates – all of them ultimately used – including Declan, Brendan, Kevin, Aidan, Finbarr, Colman, Ronan, Malachy, Jarlath and Felim, to name but a few. Each plane was formally "christened" before it made its maiden flight. They were even blessed in an annual ceremony.

It wasn't long before the company's fleet was being referred to as the "Flying Saints." Nor did it take long for people to notice strange airport flight announcements such as "St. Brigid is now leaving for Paris" or "St. Patrick has arrived from London." One Irish wag suggested that, with the way things were going, the airline should adopt the slogan "Fly with the Saints," but that was speedily rejected.

In 1947, the first *St. Brigid* – a Constellation – was on its way from Burbank, California, to take up duties with the airline. Three planes arrived that day at Shannon Airport – the *St. Brigid*, *St. Patrick* and *St. Brendan*. They flew so quickly, and landed so far ahead of schedule, that official guests missed their arrival.

Hundreds of enthusiastic Dubliners didn't make the same mistake when the *St. Brigid* Constellation flew on to Dublin. Despite a bus strike, they turned out at the old Collinstown Airport, where they saw the plane make a perfect landing. They were then permitted to view the aircraft on the airport apron. The other two planes – the *St. Patrick* and *St. Brendan* – remained at Shannon.

Less than a decade later, in 1954, another *St. Brigid* – this time a brand-new Viscount – arrived at Dublin Airport. Once again, she landed in tandem with her new sister ship, the *St. Patrick*. Thousands of sightseers turned out to greet them. One of the planes gave a demonstration flight over the city at 2.15 pm; the other did so at 4 pm.

Later, during testing and training, the Viscounts burst two tyres while landing and taking off. "We are inclined to wonder how it can happen in machines of such new design," a reporter with a national daily remarked, adding somewhat drily: "It is better that these things should happen in training flights than that they should arise in scheduled service."

The first of the Boeing 720s arrived in the early 1960s. They turned out to be excellent aircraft and great achievers. In 1962, the Boeing named after St. Brigid set a new trans-Atlantic commercial air speed record to Shannon, beating the previous record held by TWA by 17 minutes.

On that same flight the *St. Brigid* also set a new record between New York and Dublin, chipping 29 minutes off the old record. Its proud boast was that, in achieving this new land-mark time to Dublin, it had beaten the old record-holder, the *St. Patrick*, hands down!

A little later came the Boeing 707s, which were to transport Jacqueline Kennedy to Ireland. No matter what saints these planes were named after, they couldn't escape the mark of St. Brigid. Since 1966, all of them, including the *St. Patrick*, were fitted with specially-designed, deep-pile, all-wool carpets inspired by her.

The carpets featured a pattern of small St. Brigid's Crosses in grey on a background of two shades of green. Exclusively designed and manufactured by Youghal Carpets, they were chosen after months of consultation with the company's chief designer, Cormac Mehegan. All passengers, including Jacqueline Kennedy, sat with St. Brigid at their feet.

As for the former First Lady and her Irish holiday, it came to an end on 20 July 1967. She departed Woodstown House, County Waterford, shortly after 10 am, to retrace her steps to Shannon Airport for her return trip to America. Before leaving Woodstown, her children, Caroline and John, paid a visit to local shopkeeper Mary Morrissey to say their goodbyes. The family then left by car, their luggage ferried separately in a red CIE removal van.

Waiting for them at Shannon was the Aer Lingus "Flying Saint" that would carry them home. "Goodbye, thank you very much. You have all been very kind and we had a lovely summer. We all hope to be back again soon," a bronzed Jackie, dressed in the same powder blue mini-coat she wore on arrival, told the 1,000 or so well-wishers who had turned up to bid her goodbye.

She then boarded the aircraft, along with her children and two one-month-old kittens given to them by their late father's cousin when they had visited the Kennedy ancestral home in County Wexford. After a quick wave from the door, she entered what turned out to be not the *St. Brigid* but another of the airline's "saintly" aircrafts, the *St. Senan*. St. Brigid, it seems, was otherwise engaged that day!

The County Waterford village of Kilrossanty, located at the foot of the Comeragh Mountains, has a unique connection with St. Brigid dating down through the centuries. Even today, it is a thriving centre of devotion to the saint.

There is a St. Brigid's holy well in Kilrossanty, a St. Brigid's parish church and a St. Brigid's parish hall. St. Brigid is the patron saint of the parish, and the national school crest is a St. Brigid's Cross. The GAA club plays at Páirc Naomh Bríd. And that's not to mention the ruins of an old pre-Reformation church dedicated to the saint.

It's not as if the village supporting all this intense devotion is sizeable; it's actually tiny. The population of Kilrossanty was 139 in 1851, although the outlying hinterland added many thousands to its size. The village population fell to 103 in 1861, and by 1891 it had dropped to 77. Even today, it remains small. Once the surrounding area is added in, however, there are few places that can match such intense reverence for the saint.

Kilrossanty's connections with St. Brigid are linked to the local terrain. "In the parish of Kilrossanty in Waterford, there is a valley into which several glens converge, each carrying a stream from the surrounding mountains," we are told by P. W. Joyce, the Irish place-name expert, in a major study he published in 1875. These convergences – or *comars* – provided the local mountains with their name: the Comeraghs.

It was to the Comeraghs that Brigid came in 479. Local tradition holds that her arrival followed a visit made by St. Declan. He had caused chaos in the area. Not only did he upset people during a celebratory dinner, but in a fury he had caused an avalanche of rocks to fall on the surrounding fertile fields. Brigid, it seems, made a far better impression.

"Being a different kind of person, Brigid said she'd try to mitigate some of the damage," local historian Síle Murphy explains regarding the legend. "The place was littered with rocks. She said the land around the rocks would be twice as fertile as the bare fields, so that twice as much grass or crops would grow around the rocks. That was one of the gifts she gave to Kilrossanty.

"Another gift she gave was that people in Kilrossanty would never be struck by lightning. To this day, that is a big belief in the parish. In the 1950s, if I'm right, the tower of the Protestant church was struck but, as far as I know, we've never had anyone hit by lightning. You'd hear elsewhere of cattle being killed or people out on football fields being hit, but not in Kilrossanty.

"As a result, there has always been devotion to Brigid. A lot of girls who are baptized would have Brigid attached to their names. There would be Breda, Bridget and Bríd. There would be Bid and Biddy. Of course, if the girl was born in February, she would be given some variation of Brigid. She might get it as a second name. It would also go down through the family, and it still lives on."

Down through the centuries, the feast day of St. Brigid has been a high point in the Kilrossanty parish calendar. "That day is taken very seriously," Síle Murphy remarks. "It's so serious that it's a closed day for the school. Back 50 years ago, people didn't go to work. The only thing is that we always said that

Brigid brought the snow, and the Comeragh Mountains never had a St. Brigid's Day without a covering of snow.

"I remember going out collecting rushes and looking for good strong green ones that you could make your crosses with. The night before St. Brigid's Day, we'd put out a scarf, a tie or a ribbon, or something like that, for the Brat Bhríde. You'd leave that outside the door, on the windowsill or someplace. Children still love to do that today. We'd use the Brat Bhríde to cure headaches or put it around your throat to cure sore throats."

Cures have also been linked to St. Brigid's holy well, which is located close to the village. One of three wells set together in a field – the others are to the Blessed Virgin and Jesus – it attracts widespread devotion and its powers have been widely noted.

In June 1841, the eminent Ordnance Survey researcher, John O'Donovan, remarked that St. Brigid's well was beating the Blessed Virgin's well hands down. "They are seventeen paces asunder," he remarked, "and it is curious that St. Bridget's, which lies to the north, is considered to be more efficacious than the other!"

Even today, cures are reported. "A lot of people will tell you they had miracles," says Síle Murphy, who once taught at and was principal of the local school. "There was one child in first class at school and she had been hearing stories I was telling them about Brigid's miracles.

"She had warts on her face, all around her mouth. She went up to the holy wells and the next morning there was blood all over her pillow. The warts had fallen off. There are other people who cured their eyes. People would wash their eyes and they were better. People have always believed in the power of the well. That's why they visit it."

Over time, the village has also been blessed with some remarkable parish priests, most notably the Rev. Richard Power, who built the present St. Brigid's church in 1840. He was an exemplary pastor and preached eloquently in Irish. He was also an inventor of note. "He invented an improved plough, an ingenious method of propelling a boat by paddles operated by one pair of hands and some other such things," we are told in a history of the United Dioceses of Waterford and Lismore, published in 1937.

To instruct and edify his parishioners, he trained two young men to deliver presentations of religious texts from either side of the altar at Sunday Mass. Aware of the literacy and poverty levels prevailing at the time, when anything of special interest to his flock appeared in the weekly newspaper he had it read to the people in the church after Mass. It was delivered by one of his young men, who stood on a chair outside the altar rails.

Today, the parishioners of Kilrossanty still head to the church in large numbers to pay their respects to St. Brigid. They also visit St. Brigid's well. And, of course, her feast day is always well observed. More notably, the feeling persists that the village, set in the shadows of the Comeragh Mountains, with nearby whispering waterfalls and green valleys, is somehow specially blessed by the protection of a saint who visited so long ago.

"Anyone who went to school in Kilrossanty will never forget St. Brigid," Síle Murphy concludes. "We have always placed so much emphasis on her. We have so much involvement with the feast day itself. Having the day off from school, of course, helps. But we'd be very possessive of St. Brigid. We thought for a long time that she was just our saint in Kilrossanty; then we heard of places like Kildare. But I suppose that's what she always will be – our patron saint!"

This final story concerns two young Irish women named Bridget, who lived in New York in the 1960s. Their shared names, and other connections, drove American government officials to distraction.

Bridget O'Connor moved from Ballyvaughan, County Clare, to America in the early 1960s. Her father was named Michael, her sister was named Margaret, and she settled down in Manhattan. No doubt it was difficult to be so far from home but, then again, there were birthdays to celebrate, and they occurred on 20 January.

Another Bridget O'Connor also moved to America from County Clare, but this time from Milltown Malbay. She, too, had a father named Michael, a sister named Margaret, and she settled in Manhattan. No doubt it also must have been difficult for her to be so far from home but, then again, she had birthdays to celebrate, and they occurred on 20 January.

To further complicate matters, both Bridgets were mistakenly assigned identical Social Security numbers – 079-32-1780 – which tracked their earnings histories. This, in turn, caused nightmares for the two young ladies. The Ballyvaughan Bridget encountered difficulties securing her 1966 Federal income tax refund because the Internal Revenue Service couldn't establish which Bridget she was.

The Milltown Malbay Bridget was having problems with Social Security because they said she had listed herself as two people. "Social Security wrote me that somebody else was using my number. They were very upset," she said. She telephoned them. Having gone through her family details, the harried official, who couldn't believe what he was hearing, said, "Don't call us. We'll get in touch." He hurriedly hung up.

The story, when it surfaced, made news in America. The tabloid press in New York covered it. So, too, did newspapers extending from the industrial hub of New Jersey to the orange groves of California. Celebrated columnists such as Norton Mockridge – famous for answering "You think I'd make it up?" when asked if his name was real – and Joseph Cassidy of New York's *Daily News* both applied their pens to it.

Mockridge was reminded of a story he had come across about six months before. "It puts me in mind of a case that occurred in Pennsylvania last July, but which was so unbelievable I didn't tell you about it," he wrote in his column. He had become acquainted with the story – a real "puzzler," he called it – through an article in the *Greensburg Tribune-Review*.

A clerk in the Westmoreland County Common Pleas Court had written out a note which read: "I need a blotter" and handed it to Mrs. Mary Lacey, the court assistant. Misunderstanding the nature of the request, Mrs. Lacey immediately went out into the courthouse corridor and began shouting, "Ineeda Blotter! Ineeda Blotter!" just as she would when calling any witness.

People laughed at her and wondered if she had flipped her wig. Much to their surprise, within a minute or so, a young woman walked up to Mrs. Lacey and asked her what she wanted. "Hi, Ineeda," Mrs. Lacey said. "Judge Keim wants to see you." Ineeda said she couldn't imagine why the judge wanted her, and so Mrs. Lacey checked with the clerk. The clerk cleared up the mess, saying that the judge had only wanted a blotter to replace one that was soiled and torn.

Mockridge, who was intrigued by what he called a coincidence "so long that you just can't hardly believe it," decided to check out the details. He telephoned Mrs. Lacey, who explained that there was, indeed, an Ineeda Blotter, and they had both lived near each other. They had met when Mrs. Lacey was working as an election registration official and Ineeda had come in to vote.

Having put down her name as "Ineeda Blotter," Mrs. Lacey had laughed and questioned her about it. "My last name's Blotter, and my first name's Ineeda," the woman angrily replied. "What's so funny about that?" Afterwards, the two came to know each other pretty well.

It transpired that, at birth, Ineeda had been named Anita but a clerk had mistakenly written down her name as Ineeda. The name stuck. Initially there was no problem as her surname was Johnson. Eventually, however, she married a man named Blotter, which apparently raised quite a few laughs. As all her records, including licenses, were by then in the name of Ineeda, she didn't bother to change them back.

"All of this is coincidental enough, of course, but the coincidence was enormously compounded by the fact that Mrs.

Blotter happened to be in the courthouse on business the day that the clerk wrote out his note," Mockridge wrote. "Mrs. Lacey had happened to see her in the corridor just before she went in to work in the courtroom and so when she was handed a scrawled note that read: 'I need a blotter,' she naturally thought her friend was being summoned as a witness."

Mockridge also discovered that Ineeda had moved to either California or Florida – Mrs. Lacey wasn't sure which – where she planned to start a new life. "She'd always wanted to go there anyway," Mrs. Lacey told him. She intended, when she got there, to change her name back to Anita.

Regarding the two Bridgets, it was another columnist – Joseph Cassidy of New York's *Daily News* – who tracked the full story down. He even went and met the two ladies. One worked for the Archdiocese of New York, he discovered. The other worked for Schenley Industries, a liquor company based in New York with headquarters in the Empire State Building.

He found out that the two Bridgets knew each other and had just celebrated their joint birthdays at the Old Seidelberg Restaurant on New York's Third Avenue. Both were puzzled by the government's confusion over their names. "We don't even look alike," they remarked, which was correct as the income tax Bridget had soft dark hair, while the Social Security Bridget's head was covered with luxuriant flaming red tresses.

Cassidy was relieved to hear that the conundrum of their coinciding names might soon be resolved by a pending marriage. The name change would obviously sort matters out, he thought.

That was until he was told that the Ballyvaughan Bridget was about to marry the brother of the Milltown Malbay Bridget.

So, yes, from then on, Bridget O'Connor's new name would be – Bridget O'Connor! As Norton Mockridge said, "Every once in a while the long arm of coincidence is SO long that you just can't hardly believe it."

ACKNOWLEDGEMENTS

It was once said that the story of St. Brigid "pealed down the ages like bells in a cathedral tower." That image captures, with lyrical accuracy, the wonderful hymns and life stories relating to Brigid which have been chronicled, sung, translated, transcribed, and passed from one generation to the next, before reaching us today.

We are fortunate that so many of Brigid's contemporaries and near-contemporaries recorded her life. St. Brendan wrote about her. So, too, did the poet-saints Columcille and Kilian. St. Ninnid, her priest and confessor, composed a hymn to her. St. Fiech, who wrote the metrical life of St. Patrick, did so, too.

Within a century of her death, the monk Cogitosus – who most likely lived at her Kildare monastery – sat down and chronicled the highlights of her life. He covered a wide canvas, including her miracles and cures, monastic life at Kildare, and the control she exercised over monasteries elsewhere in Ireland.

Later texts, such as the *Book of Lismore*, *Leabhar Breac*, *Annals of Tigernach*, *Annals of Inisfallen*, *Leabhar Imuinn*, were priceless resources. So, also, was the ancient *Liber Hymnorum*, whose hymn to St. Brigid, composed in Old Irish, was sung by monks in the dark ages. The *Bethu Brigte*, which was written largely in Irish in the ninth century, told us the story of her ordination as a bishop.

Also of importance were the *Annals of the Four Masters*, a compilation of earlier manuscripts which was put together in the 17th century in County Donegal. Add in the writings of Gerald of Wales, who visited Kildare in the 12th century, and you end up with a fine collection of research sources. Without them, not only would this book not have been possible, but the numerous studies of St. Brigid written down through the centuries would never have got off the ground.

The Abbess of Kildare has always attracted biographers. Some notable texts have been published over the years. We are particularly indebted to the great Laois-born scholar and priest, the Rev. John O'Hanlon, whose *Lives of the Irish Saints* was published in 1875. More than three decades later, in 1907, the Rev. J. A. Knowles published his *St. Brigid, Patroness of Ireland*, which was also impressive.

In 1933, at the height of the depressed 1930s, Alice Curtayne published her biography *St. Brigid of Ireland*, which was well received. Somewhat later, during World War II, another comprehensive study of St. Brigid was produced by the English-born Irish journalist Hugh de Blacam. Titled *The Saints of Ireland: The Life Stories of S.S. Brigid and Columcille*, it also was valuable to us as a reference source.

Inevitably, many autobiographies and biographies proved useful, most notably in the case of Brigitte Bardot. Her book *Tears of Battle: An Animal Rights Memoir*, Glenys Roberts' *Bardot*, Ginette Vincendeau's *Brigitte Bardot* and Barnett Singer's *Brigitte Bardot: A Biography* chronicled her story. Official French statistics established the popularity of her name, while *Paris Match*, *Elle* and *France Today* filled in many gaps.

Other memoirs and autobiographical texts included Maud Gonne MacBride's *A Servant of the Queen*, Lady Gregory's *Seventy Years*, Bridget Hitler's *The Memoirs of Bridget Hitler*, Brendan Behan's *Confessions of an Irish Rebel*, and *The Nun of Kenmare: An Autobiography*. The Nun of Kenmare also published *Cloister Songs and Hymns for Children* under her religious name, Sr. Mary Francis Clare.

Of the numerous other texts consulted for this book, some deserve to be singled out. They include *Pirate Queen: The Life of Grace O'Malley*, by Judith Cook, *Grace O'Malley: The Biography of Ireland's Pirate Queen*, by Anne Chambers, *Kathleen Lynn: Irishwoman, Patriot, Doctor*, by Margaret Ó hÓgartaigh, and *Lockout Dublin 1913*, by Pádraig Yeates.

Among others were *The Catholics of Ireland under the Penal Laws in the 18th Century*, published in 1899 and written by Cardinal Moran, *The Bardic Stories of Ireland*, which was issued in 1871 and written by Patrick Kennedy, *The House of Cromwell and the Story of Dunkirk*, by James Waylen and published in 1880, and *Cromwell: Our Chief of Men*, by Antonia Fraser.

Regarding Brigid's visit to Scotland, of great value was the article *St. Brigid and St. Bride in Scotland*, by Heather Upfield, which is available online. Another online article, which is also excellent, was Rita Minehan's *From the Acorn to the Oak: Celebrating the Brigidine Story*. One final, but very important, source was Thomas Johnson Westropp's contribution regarding Clare Island and Grace O'Malley to the *Clare Island Survey*, which again can be accessed online.

Background information to the extraordinary celebrations surrounding Garland Sunday at Liscannor and Lahinch was contained in *The Festival of Lughnasa*, by Máire MacNeill, and *Flowing Tides*, by Gearóid Ó hAllmhuráin. Given the wild festivities that sometimes surrounded the occasion, participants might have been interested in *A History of Beer and Brewing*, by Ian S. Hornsey, which was valuable to us in relation to Brigid's brewing activities.

Nothing attracted more attention in Victorian times than gardening, and few gardeners were more popular than Alice Louisa Lawrenson. Stories about her anemones and Christmas Roses cropped up everywhere, including in the *Gardeners' Chronicle* and *Garden* magazine. They also appeared in recent publications of the Irish Garden Plant Society, some of which were written by the botanist, Charles Nelson. The testimonial to Lawrenson from Frederick W. Burbidge appeared in the *Journal of Horticulture*.

Many other journals were a valued source of information. The *Irish Monthly* was not only helpful in explaining the story of the Brigidine Sisters, but it also provided us with that late 19th-century description by "M. McG" of the shrine at Faughart. Other journals of note included *The Month*, *Irish Digest* and the *Irish Rosary*.

Special mention must be made of *The Journal of the Royal Society of Antiquaries of Ireland*, which in 1987 published a priceless article titled Cogitosus's "Life of St. Brigit" Content and Value, by Sean Connolly and J.-M. Picard. The article detailed the life of Cogitosus, and it also provided a translation of part of his *Life of Saint Brigit*. The layout and content of their study is excellent.

Also of importance were the *Journal of the Waterford and South-East of Ireland Archaeological Society, Journal of the County Kildare Archaeological Society, Ulster Journal of Archaeology, Journal of the County Louth Archaeological and Historical Society, Irish Historical Studies*, and *Irish Ecclesiastical Record*.

Many Irish newspapers were also consulted, among them the *Irish Independent, Sunday Independent, Irish Press, Irish Times, Cork Examiner, Sunday Tribune, Nation, Freeman's Journal, Evening Herald, Evening Echo*, Dublin's *Daily Express* and *Evening Telegraph, Belfast News Letter, Belfast Telegraph*, and *Irish Citizen*.

Local and provincial publications included the *Northern Whig, Dundalk Democrat, Connacht Tribune, Waterford News and Star, Ballina Herald, Leinster Leader, Westmeath Independent, Westmeath Examiner, Meath Chronicle*, and *Connaught Telegraph*.

Also of note were the *Western People, Nenagh Guardian, Strabane Chronicle, Ulster Herald, Donegal Democrat, Donegal News, Derry People and Tirconaill News, Fermanagh Herald, Tuam Herald, Leinster Express*, and *Kildare Observer*.

Others of importance were the *Sligo Champion, Munster Express, Longford Leader, Drogheda Independent, Anglo-Celt, Leitrim Observer, Kerry News, Kerryman, Kerry Sentinel, Kerry Evening Post, Kerry Weekly Reporter, Wexford People, Derry Journal, Limerick Leader, Liberator* (Tralee), *Connacht Sentinel, Irish Catholic*, and *Nationalist and Leinster Times*.

Brigid's visit to Glastonbury surfaced in far too many publications for us to list. We must, however, single out a paper, St. Brigid and Glastonbury, by the Ven. Archdeacon John L. Robinson, published by the Royal Society of Antiquaries of Ireland in 1953. *Irish Saints in Great Britain*, by Patrick Francis Moran, published in 1879, was also useful, as was Brian Wright's excellent *Brigid: Goddess, Druidess and Saint* regarding the discovery of Brigid's handbell.

The *Central Somerset Gazette* was vital to our Glastonbury research. Other British newspapers of note included the *Globe*, *Pall Mall Gazette*, *Westminster Gazette*, *Daily Express*, *Daily Mirror*, *Reynolds's Newspaper*, *John Bull*, *Manchester Evening News*, *Daily News*, *Leicester Daily Post*, *Lancashire Evening Post*, *Orkney Herald*, *Scotsman*, *Times* of London, *Glamorgan Gazette*, *Daily Citizen*, *Suffragette*, and *Votes for Women*.

Turning to North America, New York's *Daily News* and the *Knoxville Journal* were especially useful in the war bride story, while the *Daily News*, *Paterson Evening News*, *Redlands Daily Facts*, and *Greensburg Tribune-Review* provided the basis for the story of the two County Clare Bridgets featured at the end of the book. The *New York Times* and *Boston Pilot* were also important.

The *St. Louis Globe-Democrat*, *Time-Picayune*, *Western Home Journal*, and New York's *Evening World* described the adventures of Fr. Thomas Mooney during the American Civil War. Another great resource for that story was *The Irish Brigade and its Campaigns*, by David Power Conyngham, published in 1867.

Other newspapers from America included the *San Francisco Examiner*, *San Francisco Call*, *Memphis Appeal*, *Buffalo Daily Republic*, *Austin Daily Herald*, *Napa Journal*, *Barre Daily Times*, *Kenosha News*, *Great Falls Daily Tribune*, and *Sioux City Journal*.

Many people deserve credit for their help with this book, most notably Ethna Fitzgerald, who suggested the idea in the first place. We also extend our sincere thanks to Oriana Conner for permission to use the poem by Winifred Letts, which is featured at the top of the book, and to Bairbre O'Hogan for her assistance. Professor Con Timon, along with Linda Monahan and Barbara Ryan of Typeform, were invaluable, as always.

Kevin McCarthy, from Cappoquin, and Professor Pádraig Ó Macháin, from UCC, were most helpful in untangling the authorship of an ancient hymn to St. Brigid. Edel Gannon, of Crosscare, was equally supportive in sorting out issues relating to St. Brigid's Penny Dinners. The libraries of Dun Laoghaire, Dungarvan and Waterford, along with Clare County Library, couldn't have been more obliging.

We are also grateful to two good friends, Dorothea and Jeremy, for their encouragement and support. Additional thanks to John Daly, who introduced us to Seán and Síle Murphy, both of whom proved so helpful with our Kilrossanty story. Pat Collender also provided encouragement and advice during our visit to Kilrossanty village.

Paddy Carey, Michael and Patricia Manahan, and Hugh and Mags Coogan were of more help than they can imagine. So, also, were Nicholas Connors and Neilus O'Donoghue in our hour of need.

Lastly, our thanks to St. Brigid, whose character emerged into the light, and whose personality came to life, during the writing of this book. "Strong in affection, ready in pity, clear in judgement, bright in spirit," it was once said of her. But she had a lot more to offer than that. Few could match her kindness, warmth and affection. For those reasons alone, she turned out to be a wonderful person to write about.

WE'LL MEET AGAIN

IRISH DEATHBED VISIONS
WHO YOU MEET WHEN YOU DIE

Colm Keane

We do not die alone. That's the remarkable conclusion of this extraordinary book examining deathbed visions.

Parents, children, brothers, sisters and close friends who have already died are among those who return to us as we pass away. Religious figures appear to others, while more see visions of beautiful landscapes.

Riveting case histories are featured, along with numerous stories from those left behind who describe after-death visitations and many other strange occurrences. The latest scientific evidence is discussed.

We'll Meet Again, written by award-winning journalist Colm Keane, is one of the most challenging books ever compiled on this intriguing theme.

Reviews of *We'll Meet Again*

'A total page-turner' *Cork 103 FM*
'Packed with riveting case histories' *LMFM Radio*
'A fascinating book' *Limerick's Live 95FM*

HEADING FOR THE LIGHT

THE 10 THINGS THAT HAPPEN WHEN YOU DIE

Colm Keane

This explosive book reveals the truth about what happens when we die.

The ten stages we go through when we die are outlined for the very first time. They establish conclusively that death is a warm, happy experience and is nothing to fear.

Based on five years of research, the author has drawn from the real-life stories of people who have temporarily died and returned to life.

This definitive book provides you with all you need to know about the stages of death as we head for the light.

Reviews of *Heading for the Light*

'Absolutely fascinating' *RTÉ One*
'Provides much pause for thought' *Sunday Independent*
'The mysteries of dying and death from those who know'
The Irish Catholic

Capel Island Press
Baile na nGall, Ring, Dungarvan,
County Waterford, Ireland
Email: capelislandpress@hotmail.com